The
WATLINGTON
BRANCH

by

J.S. Holden, M.A.

Oxford Publishing Co

When the Watlington Branch of the former Great Western system closed to passenger traffic at the end of June 1957, my awareness of railways was confined to the short stretch of the "Met. and Great Central Joint" on which I travelled daily. I am therefore particularly grateful to all the ex-employees and local residents whose recollections of the line I have been able to call upon, and would like to thank individually those who also loaned or donated photographs and other material: retired driver Harry Humphries and stationmen Charlie Hopkins and Tom Tunnicliffe, Mrs. Clarke and Mrs. Tate, who allowed use to be made of the memoirs of their father, the late Mr. R.H. Pocock, stationmaster at Watlington, Mr. & Mrs. A.J. Scott, Mr. R.H. Siarey, and Geoff Gamble, who provided all the diesel-era pictures and details of the present-day operation of the line.

I am indebted to the Chinnor Cement and Lime Co. and Mr. E.G. Tappin for information on, respectively, cement and coal traffic, and to the Hon. J. Parker for permission to take the measurements on which the drawings of Watlington station are based.

The assistance of the County Record Offices at Aylesbury and Oxford in allowing access to maps and Acts of Parliament, and of the Great Western Railway Museum at Swindon in permitting the reproduction of Company seals is gratefully acknowledged; as is the co-operation of the staff of the Transport Records, Porchester Road, British Railways Public Relations Department at Paddington and Photographic Section at Swindon, and of fellow members of the H.M.R.S. Ross Pochin, Jack Slinn, Colin Strevens, and Dick Riley.

Thanks are also due to my father who helped considerably with photographic work, to my brother James, who did a major part of the research, read the manuscript and subjected me to a constructive barrage of suggestions and criticism, and finally to my wife Pam, not only for showing forbearance over the whole project and assisting with the typing, but also for actively participating in the gathering of material.

Printed by B.H. Blackwell (Printing) in the City of Oxford

Photo reproduction by Oxford Litho Plates Limited.

SBN 0 902888 41 2

Published by
Oxford Publishing Co.,
5 Lewis Close, Risinghurst, Oxford.

CHAPTER I

The Wallingford and Watlington Railway

Watlington in the middle years of the nineteenth century was an unremarkable town of a little under two thousand inhabitants. Located below the ridge of the Chiltern Hills, a settlement was known to exist there from the sixth century. By the fourteenth century the town was of sufficient stature for a market and annual fair to be granted, and much of the modern streetplan has remained unaltered from that time. By the seventeenth century, Watlington had a greater population than the other rural parishes of South Oxfordshire.

It thus became the natural centre of a predominantly agricultural area bounded by the River Thames to the west, and the towns of Thame to the north, High Wycombe in the east, and Henley to the southeast. Despite its potential, Watlington failed to achieve the importance of these other towns and for this poor communications were largely to blame. Local roads were described as "probably the worst in the Country", and the nearest navigable waterway was the Thames six miles distant at Wallingford. It is not surprising that by the 1860's, when railways already stretched much of the length and breadth of the Country, the local landowners of Watlington looked to this new form of transport as a means of bringing the agricultural produce of their estates to expanding markets in the cities, and with it, prosperity to themselves and the town.

A connection by way of Wallingford to the Great Western Railway, whose main line from London to Bristol was no more than nine miles away, was the first choice of the promotors. The Great Western had opened the section of its line between Reading and Steventon as long previously as June 1840, and the branch from a junction at Didcot to Oxford in the same month of 1844. A railway linking Watlington and Wallingford to the London-Bristol main line offered the prospect of excellent communications with these two cities, and also with the Midlands via Oxford and Didcot.

An alternative to this scheme, worthy of at least some consideration by the Watlington representatives, would have been a connection with the Wycombe Railway, whose line joined the Great Western at Maidenhead thereby allowing through traffic to London. Access to the Midlands would also have been assured once the Wycombe company's extension beyond Thame was completed: the opening to Kennington Junction near Oxford took place in late October of the year in which the Wallingford and Watlington Railway Act passed through Parliament.

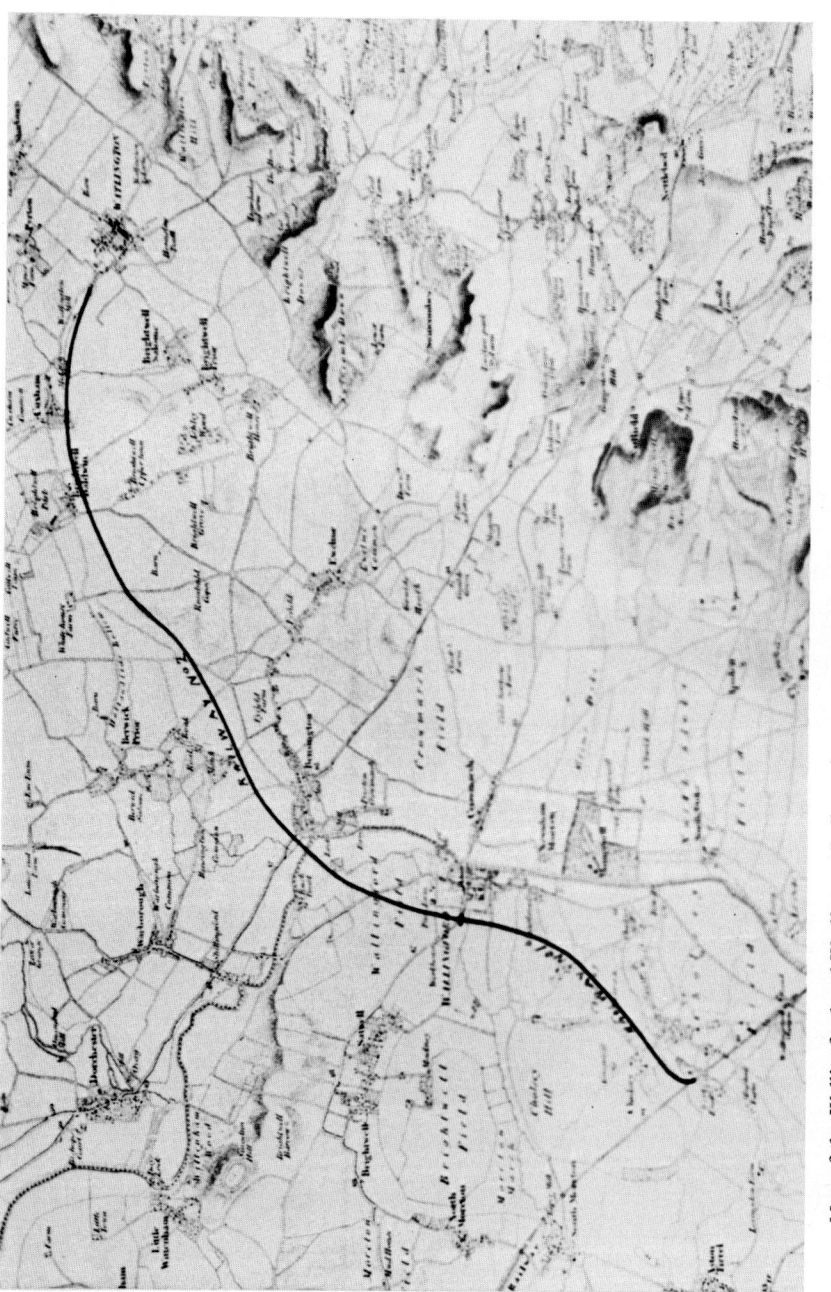

Map of the Wallingford and Watlington Railway from the original Parliamentary deposition. The Great Western main line can be seen running diagonally across the lower left hand corner. Wallingford Road station appears some distance to the London side of the junction, and near the Thames which can be traced northwards past Wallingford, Bensington and Dorchester. *(Courtesy Oxfordshire County Council)*

There were, however, disadvantages to this alternative, the most significant being the absence of anywhere of comparable importance to Wallingford between Watlington and a junction with the Wycombe Railway capable of generating traffic on the line and capital to build it. The Wycombe Railway was also a far from ideal link, as it was then worked solely on the broad gauge and could not be claimed to have anything other than branch line status.

The Wallingford and Watlington Railway was promoted by an Act of Parliament in the Session of 1864. The Act empowered the construction of a railway from a junction with the Great Western Railway in the Parish of Cholsey, near to the milepost denoting 48½ miles from London. It was to terminate near the turnpike road from Wallingford to Wantage "about one hundred and thirty yards to the westward of the Cross Keys Public House" in Wallingford. A second railway was to make an end-on connection with Railway No. 1, as it was named, and terminate in a field known as the Upper Moor Meadow near the Watlington to Oxford road at Watlington.

The working of the line by the Great Western was clearly envisaged, and due provision was made for this in the Act. Clause 24 permitted the rails to be laid to broad, narrow (i.e. standard) gauge, or both. In the event, the narrow gauge only was laid. Mixed gauge had been laid on the Great Western between Oxford and Reading by the end of 1856 and, although steps to abolish the broad gauge were not implemented until 1869, the ultimate fate of Brunel's gauge must have been evident by the mid 1860's. The Wallingford and Watlington Railway thus became the first narrow gauge branch out of the original G.W.R. main line. The authorised capital was eight thousand shares of £10 each, with borrowing powers for a further £26,000 once the capital was fully subscribed. The original Directors were William Hawes, Edward Poole, and James Childs.

The contractor for the line was a Mr. Thomas White whose tender of £20,232 for the construction of Railway No. 1, exclusive of Wallingford station, was accepted in December 1864. In the following March, the Directors resolved to obtain a tender from Mr. White for the continuation of the line across the Thames to Bensington (Benson). Subsequently, Mr. Childs agreed to take a further 400 shares and use his influence among his friends to raise the necessary funds for the extension on condition that he become Chairman: William Hawes duly stood down.

Shortly after, in June, a Mr. Peel was advised as representative of the Watlington interests, that the further extension of the line from Benson to Watlington would be commenced immediately if one thousand shares were taken in the neighbourhood and land released at no more than £150 per acre on average. A tender was also received from a Mr. James Burke for Railway No. 2. For the 1 mile and 60 chains to Bensington, this amounted to £15,452, while £16,148 was the sum for the 4 miles and 60 chains thence to Watlington. The first part was of course relatively more expensive for the distance involved because it included the Thames crossing.

Meanwhile, the construction of Railway No. 1 proceeded with such capital as had been raised, and the line was opened on July 2nd 1866 as far as the temporary terminus at Wallingford. The distance from the junction with the Great Western Railway was 3 miles and 24 chains, Wallingford Road being the junction station. This was renamed Moulsford, thereby reverting to the title by which the station had been known until late in 1840. Moulsford was superseded in 1892 by a new station called Cholsey and Moulsford, further west and closer to Wallingford. No significant works were required on the section opened and gradients were easy, falling at 1 in 102 for three furlongs from the junction and rising at 1 in 594 for seven furlongs closer to Wallingford, the rest being level. The Great Western Railway worked the branch from the outset.

Thomas White duly tendered for the first part of the extension to Watlington, the figure being £16,218 for the distance to Bensington, of which one quarter was to be in paid-up shares, as for the initial part of the line. From Wallingford, the Railway would have climbed at 1 in 165, crossing the Wallingford and Wantage Turnpike Road. After a level stretch in a cutting, the Reading, Wallingford and Oxford Turnpike was to bridge the line, which would then fall at 1 in 280 to the Thames.

The river itself was to be crossed by a viaduct with three arches each of 50 feet span, and a further two of 20 feet, all 12 feet high. This was at a point eleven furlongs from Wallingford and just upstream of Bensington Lock. The Oxford and Henley Turnpike was then to be bridged almost immediately, and the line would have swung to the east on rising gradients to a summit three miles beyond the Thames near Brightwell Baldwin. At this point it would have been 136 feet above the level of the junction with the Great Western. From here, undulating gradients, the steepest at 1 in 82, would have carried the line to a station by the Oxford road in Watlington. At

142 feet above the level of the junction, this would have been the highest point on the branch. The section to Watlington would have crossed mostly fields, several being in the ownership of Colleges of the University of Oxford. A number of dwellings appeared to have stood in the line of the Railway, and several minor roads and footpaths were to be crossed on the level.

Money for the extension was not forthcoming, however. The times were inauspicious for raising new funds following the collapse of a major firm of financiers in May of 1866. Even the seemingly immovable Great Western Railway was seriously affected by reaction against railway shares, and a number of other railways were brought to the verge of insolvency. While the worst was over by the middle of 1867, a period of austerity continued. Indeed, early in 1868 the Secretary of the Wallingford and Watlington company took a cut in salary from £80 to £60 p.a. in the search for economies to improve the financial position of the railway. From the 1st of January 1868, fares were raised. In December of that year, the Board was pressed for payment of debts to the contractor, Thomas White, and throughout the next year complaints over non-payment of outstanding sums to the contractor, the Great Western, and others were a persistent feature of meetings. It is not surprising, then, that any consideration of extension beyond Wallingford was deferred.

At the December meeting, the Directors' attention was drawn to a notice in the London Gazette of application to Parliament for a bill to authorise the construction of a railway from Watlington to Princes Risborough, of which more in the next chapter. It is not clear whether the Watlington faction in the Wallingford and Watlington company saw no hope of completion of that Railway as authorised, or whether the line to Princes Risborough was part of some grander design to form a through route. Certain it is that the Watlington stations of the two lines as promoted were about a mile apart, although there was no insuperable obstruction to prevent their subsequent connection.

There is no evidence to suggest that the Wallingford Railway took an active interest in either coming to an arrangement with the new company or fighting it in defence of a potential monopoly of rail traffic at Watlington. The only suggestion of a unifying nature that seems to have emerged was reported by the Secretary of the Great Western Railway at a Directors' meeting in March 1869. This

An interesting might-have-been. Wallingford viewed towards the buffers and in the direction of the never-realised extension to Watlington.

(Loco. and General Railway Photos)

Watlington Station. The town of Watlington is to the Southwest behind the trees in the distance, with Wallingford and the Thames six miles beyond. *(Lens of Sutton)*

proposed that the lines which had yet to be built, from Wallingford to Watlington and from there to Princes Risborough, should be abandoned and substituted by tramways running along the roads of the district. The Great Western saw no objections to negotiations to that purpose between the parties concerned.

The Wallingford company approached the G.W.R. in August 1870 with a view to vesting the line in the larger concern, a predictable move for an enterprise as impecunious as the Wallingford and Watlington. The Great Western had been working the railway since the opening, and became responsible for its maintenance as well from mid-October 1867, three months later in the event than specified by the working agreement.

Grierson, representing the G.W.R., adopted an attitude which was later repeated with the Watlington and Princes Risborough Railway, and which seems to have been a feature of his company's dealings with smaller neighbours. This was to express lack of interest until the neighbouring concern was in financial difficulties, when it could be purchased at a much reduced price. Grierson's reply on this occason concluded that "the balance being small, we could not make you an offer which you would be likely to accept . . . therefore we think that for the present at all events the matter had better stand over and as the traffic is somewhat improving we may be able to make you a more satisfactory proposal than we can do just now". Traffic receipts in fact fell slightly over the next year, although a reduction was made in the running deficit.

Nonetheless, negotiations were renewed with greater success in 1871, when it became clear that the Wallingford company, in difficulties over the capital for the existing line, had completely abandoned hope of building the second section to Watlington of the railway authorised in 1864. In June, broad agreement was reached with the Great Western. As part of this, the Wallingford and Watlington was to seek powers to abandon the section beyond Wallingford and rearrange and reduce their capital of which only £17,575 had been paid up. The line was then to be vested in the Great Western Railway, who were to give £3,515 5% preference shares in payment for the paid up ordinary stock of the Wallingford company, and £16,750 in cash or preference stock.

The enabling Act was put through Parliament in the Session of 1872 and the transfer was completed on the 2nd December of that year. The end of the Wallingford and Watlington's independent existence finally destroyed any remaining hope of a railway to Watlington from across the Thames. It is doubtful whether a line to the west would have fared any better in later years than the line actually built to Princes Risborough. Indeed, the Watlington extension from Wallingford might well have withered at an earlier date, as it would probably not have attracted traffic equivalent to that ultimately generated by the Chinnor lime and cement works to sustain it. A through route with the addition of a north curve to make a triangular junction at Princes Risborough could have generated more traffic on the line before the growth of motorised road transport; but it is unlikely, considering the fate of other cross-country routes, that it would have resulted in a line that was viable in terms of today's transport needs.

Proposals to create a through railway by reviving the Watlington to Wallingford section were made from time to time, but none came to fruition. It is perhaps worth mentioning one which came before the Great Western Directors in 1891. This, from Mr. James Wilkinson, engineer of the International Construction Co., asked whether the Great Western would consider working such a line if constructed, on the basis of guaranteeing 3% on capital cost estimated at £50,000. The Directors were "unable to entertain the proposal".

Seal of the Wallingford and Watlington Railway. *(Courtesy Great Western Railway Museum, Swindon)*

CHAPTER II

The Watlington and Princes Risborough Railway

We have seen how ambitions for a rail outlet from Watlington to the Great Western Railway's main line were frustrated. Once it became evident that the Wallingford and Watlington Railway was in difficulties as to the completion of its line, the Watlington interests began to look for an alternative. Clearly, capital outlay was to be kept to a minimum. Princes Risborough was therefore the obvious target for a connection with the existing railway network. Other routes would be precluded by the severe gradients necessary to cross the Chiltern Hills, by the expense of bridging the Thames, or by mere distance to the potential junction. A line to the Wycombe Railway at Risborough need be no more than nine miles long and, more important, could be built with the minimum of earthworks and engineering features.

It is worth considering briefly at this point how Princes Risborough came to be established on the railway map. The Wycombe Railway was authorised in 1846 to build a line from Maidenhead on the Great Western Railway to High Wycombe, and the Great Western authorised to purchase the railway in the following Session. Neither was put into effect and the powers lapsed, but were revived in 1852. The Wycombe Railway was opened in 1854, as a single line of cheap construction on the broad gauge, and leased to the Great Western. In August 1862, the line was extended and opened to Thame by way of Princes Risborough, which achieved junction status by the opening of the Aylesbury Branch fourteen months later. Finally, as we have seen, the Wycombe Railway reached Kennington Junction, two miles south of Oxford, from Thame in October 1864.

Princes Risborough was thus on a through route between London and the Midlands, although the Wycombe Railway section, being single track, steeply graded and broad gauge only, effectively prevented its use as such. The Wycombe Railway was absorbed by the Great Western in 1867, and powers were obtained during the Parliamentary Session of that year to reduce it to the narrow gauge, although the early conversion of this and other lines was delayed by the difficult financial situation. However, the Aylesbury branch was converted in October 1868 to avoid the expense of mixed gauge in Aylesbury station, which was to be shared with the Aylesbury and

Buckingham Railway. The remainder of the erstwhile Wycombe Railway was narrowed two years subsequently.

The Watlington and Princes Risborough Railway was promoted largely by the local landowners, rather than by any industrial or mercantile interests, and authorised in the Session of 1869 by an Act dated the 26th July. As has been noted, the Thame to Risborough line was still broad gauge, although powers for conversion had been obtained. The Act therefore had to take account of this rather awkward situation which, as it transpired, was avoided by the conversion of the Thame and Oxford line before the Watlington and Princes Risborough Railway was completed.

Powers were conferred by the Act for a railway — Railway No. 3 on the deposited plans — "commencing in the parish of Princes Risborough in the County of Buckingham by a junction with the Wycombe Railway (Thame Extension) of the Great Western Railway Company, and terminating in the parish of Pyrton in the County of Oxford near the town of Watlington." The junction between the two railways was to be constructed by the Great Western at the expense of the Watlington company "at such points and in such manner as agreed" between the engineers of the two companies.

The Great Western was obliged, before the opening of the Watlington line to "at their own cost, convert or alter into a narrow-gauge or into a mixed-gauge railway at least one line of railway on their Wycombe Railway (Thame Extension) between their Princes Risborough station and the commencement of the railway by this Act authorised". For the provision of these and station facilities, and exercise of running powers, the Watlington and Princes Risborough Railway was to pay tolls of not less than £150 p.a. For the purposes of calculating tolls, the distance was considered to be one and a half miles, although it was actually less than a mile.

The phrase "convert or alter . . . at least one line of railway" is curious, since there was only one existing line over this section. The reference is presumably to the second, parallel line — Railway No. 2 on the plans — which was built by the Great Western but not specifically mentioned in the Watlington Railway Act. There was, however, no cause for the Great Western to build this parallel line to anything but the narrow gauge in the first place, since it was solely for the use of the Watlington company and the junction arrangements as they appeared in the plans did not permit the two lines of rails to be operated in the customary "up" and "down"

Map of the Watlington and Princes Risborough Railway from the original Parliamentary deposition.
(Courtesy Oxfordshire County Council)

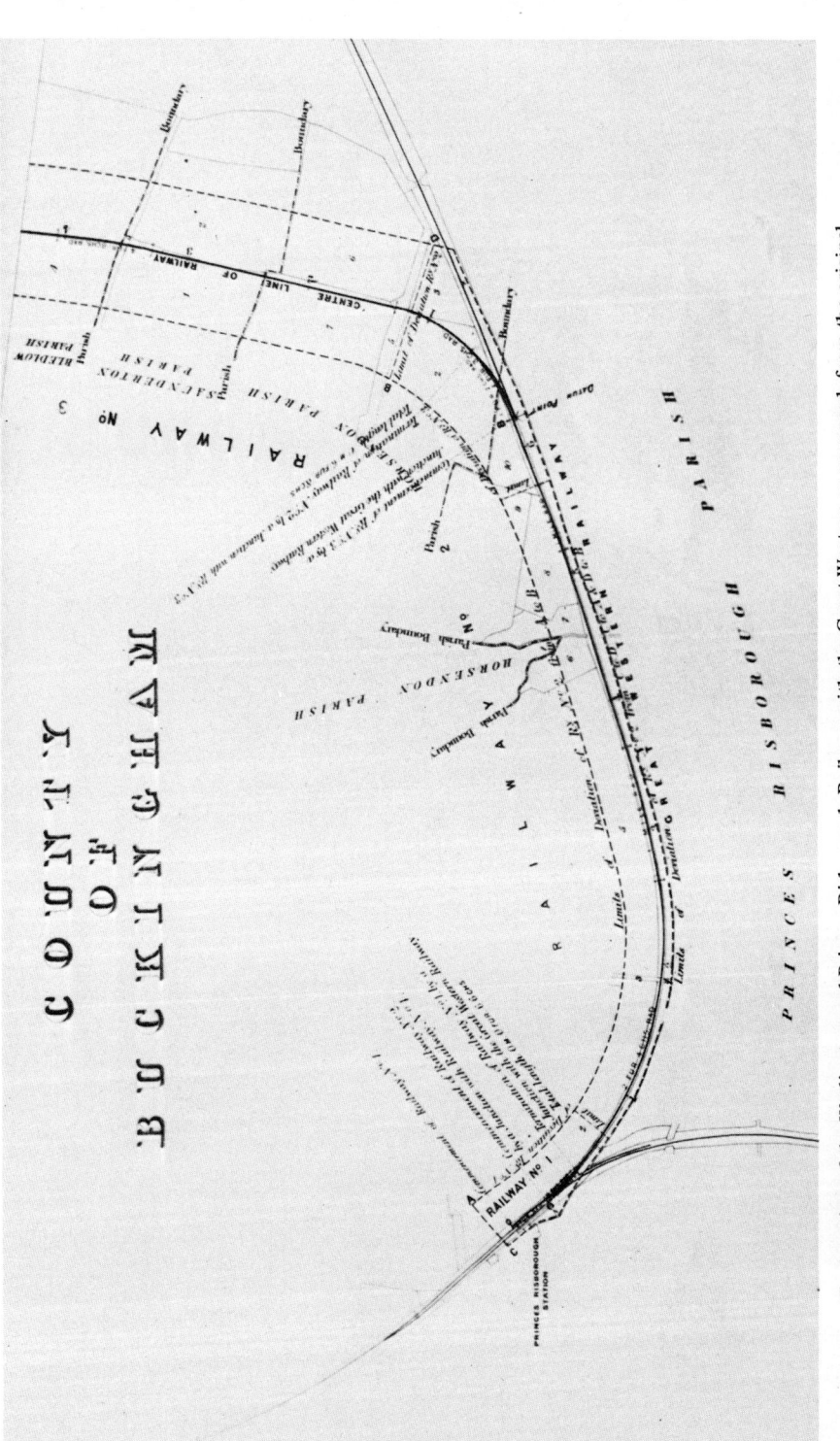

The junction of the Watlington and Princes Risborough Railway with the Great Western as proposed, from the original plans and sections *(Courtesy Oxfordshire County Council)*

manner. There would still, therefore, be only one line of the Great Western which could be converted or altered for the benefit of the newcomers. It may be presumed, incidentally, that the Watlington company regarded Railway No. 2 as something of a luxury which could be built in due course to simplify operation. Their notice of intended application for Parliamentary powers, although it sought authority for this short section, also proposed the laying of additional (narrow gauge) rails between junction and station on the existing Great Western line. These would have been unnecessary if Railway No. 2 had been considered an essential part of the original scheme of things. Gauge problems were avoided by the conversion of the Wycombe Railway, but the exercise of running powers was to cause protracted bickering between the parties.

Three Railways were distinguished in the deposited plans, of which two have already been mentioned. Railway No. 1 ran from opposite the existing platform at Risborough station to a junction with the G.W.R. roughly seventy yards beyond the north end of the platform, and beyond the junction for Aylesbury. It was 6 chains long and level. Railway No. 2 was to branch from Railway No. 1 opposite the north end of the platform, and terminate in a junction with Railway No. 3. This second line was intended to run parallel to the existing line to Thame, and adhere to much the same levels, falling at 1 in 180 and 1 in 107 away from Princes Risborough. It curved to the west over a distance of 68 chains, and encroached on fields in the ownership of Baron Rothschild and the Reverend Partridge, as well as Great Western Railway land.

Railway No. 3 curved sharply away from its intended junction with the Great Western line, to follow a southwesterly course towards Watlington. As surveyed, this line initially rose and fell on gradients no steeper than 1 in 193, crossing the road to Bledlow village on the level and passing through rolling farmland. Seven furlongs from the junction, the gradient steepened to 1 in 78, followed by three furlongs at 1 in 61 and nearly a mile at 1 in 67, all against Watlington-bound trains. A second road to Bledlow and the road to Hempton Wainhill were also to be crossed on the level in this section, the land rising sharply from near the railway at Wainhill towards the southeast and Bledlow Great Wood.

Just before the intended station at Chinnor, the gradient changed in favour of down trains, falling at 1 in 154 and 1 in 103 to a point

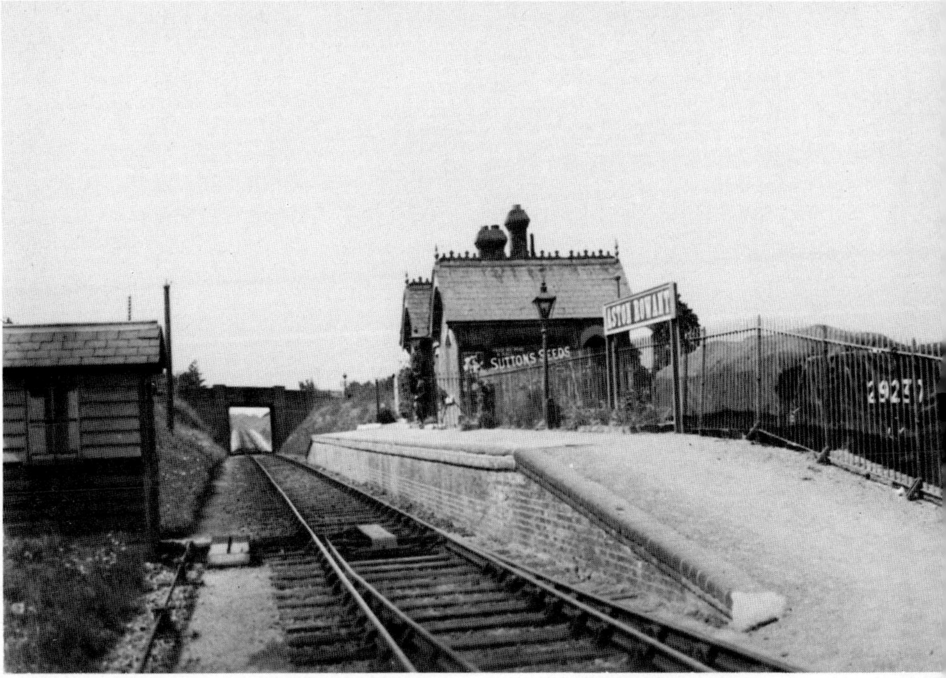

(Loco. & General Railway Photographs)

Aston Rowant Station in 1919 (above) and about 1950 (below). The bridge in the background carries the main Oxford road. *(Lens of Sutton)*

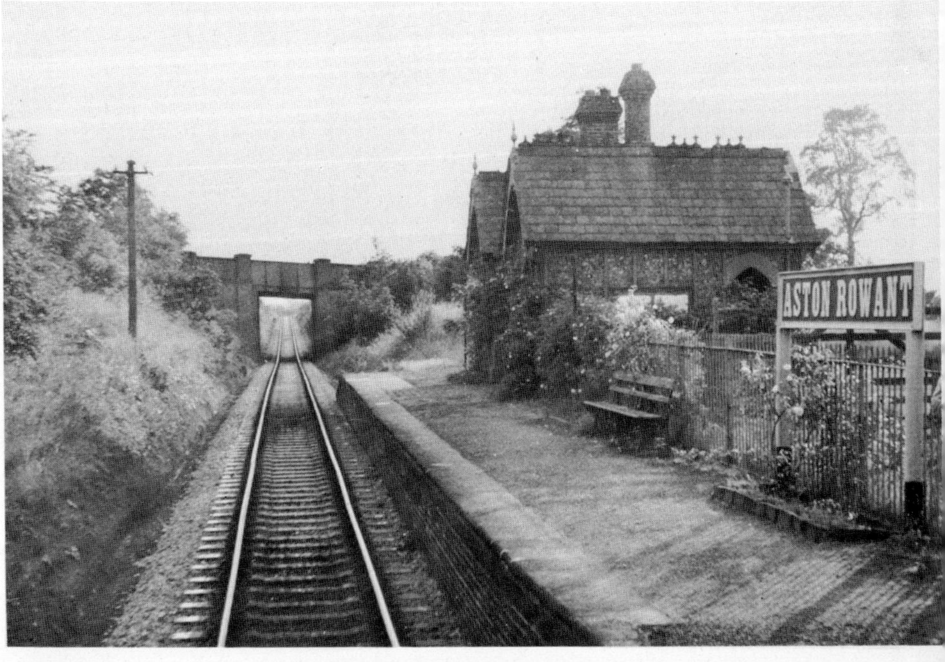

(Loco. & General Railway Photographs)

Another contrast between two post-war eras. Chinnor Station changed little: the cement works, off to the left in the earlier view, was transformed almost out of recognition. *(Lens of Sutton)*

three miles distant from the junction. The line was then to rise and fall on easy gradients for just over half a mile until, at the nearest point to the village of Crowell, the climb restarted in earnest at 1 in 85 for half a mile, followed by nearly three furlongs downhill at 1 in 75. The road from Kingston Blount through Kingston Wood was to be crossed on the level and, for the following mile, the ancient Icknield Way ran beside the projected route.

Shortly after what was later to be known as Kingston Crossing, the line again started to climb, initially at 1 in 94, to the highest point on the branch, four miles and three furlongs from the junction and 150 feet above its level. The Stokenchurch Turnpike Road — now the A40 Oxford Road — was to be crossed at this point, once again on the level, and the second intermediate station of Aston Rowant erected at the crossing. The railway here curved rather more to the west towards the village of Lewknor in order to pass to the north of a hillock called The Knapp, afterwards resuming its southwesterly course towards Watlington. Except for two furlongs rising at 1 in 113 by Lewknor, the line descended from Aston Rowant towards Watlington, initially at 1 in 105 and ultimately at 1 in 74 to a point half a mile short of the terminus.

The rising section near Lewknor contained the only bridge originally planned on the line. This, over a public road, was to be 25 feet span and 15 feet high, and be followed by the deepest cutting on the branch. Just before passing the Earl of Macclesfield's seat at Shirburn Castle on the right, the gradient changed to 1 in 115 against down trains, finally falling at 1 in 220 into the station. This was at a point 8 miles 4¾ chains from the junction, and still half a mile short of the town of Watlington.

It may be wondered why the line was not taken closer to the town, particularly as the land was almost level and only fields intervened. The reason generally advanced is that the position of the terminus was convenient for the Earl of Macclesfield at Shirburn, and was indeed a compromise site between Shirburn and Watlington. Since the Earl owned the land on which the terminus and approach were to be built, as well as the intervening fields towards Watlington, and as his estate generated much of the early traffic on the line, he was in a powerful position to influence the choice of location!

As surveyed, the branch contained only one bridge, but no less than six level crossings of public roads as well as a number of farm occupation crossings. None of these six was of any significance with the exception of the Oxford Road which, even in those days, must have carried a substantial amount of traffic. Assuming that all six were to have crossing keepers, who would have had to be paid and found accommodation, the substitution of bridges where possible was doubtless considered desirable, and was indeed made by the time the line was built. The railway bridged both roads to Bledlow, and was carried under the road at Chinnor and the Oxford Road. This left level crossings at Wainhill and Kingston, both equipped with keepers' cottages and, in Great Western days, with unstaffed halts.

The substitution of bridges led to changes in the levels, and the gradients of the line as built differed substantially from those for the line as projected. A G.W.R. gradient profile appears on page 27. The general line of the railway was unchanged, however, and the minimal earthworks evident in the original plans were scarcely increased as a result of the revised levels. There were short cuttings before Chinnor station, after Aston Rowant and near Lewknor, and short embankments over gullies at the Risborough end, but none of these amounted to more than 15-20 feet in height.

The authorised capital of the Watlington and Princes Risborough railway was £36,000 in £10 shares, with powers to raise a further £12,000 by borrowing once the share capital was fully subscribed. The first Directors, for whom the qualification was twenty shares, were Thomas Taylor, Francis Edward Stephens Viret, John Henry Westcar Peel, William Harrison Davey, and Thomas Alexander Allnutt.

Of these, only Thomas Taylor owned land which was crossed by the Railway, in the parishes of Saunderton, Bledlow and Aston Rowant, and purchases had to be arranged with a further thirty owners, excluding those connected solely with the road crossings. Most of the railway right of way was through farmland belonging to the Lords of the Manor in the various parishes. These included the Reverend Partridge in Horsenden, Lord Carington and the President of Eton College in Bledlow, the Earl of Abingdon and Baroness Wenman in Crowell, and John Brown and Thomas Taylor in Aston Rowant. Finally, beyond the Oxford Road, they were Sir Edward Joddrell in Lewknor and the Earl of Macclesfield at Shirburn.

The Great Western Railway had been prepared to petition against the Watlington and Princes Risborough Railway early in 1869. The clauses and amendments which the Great Western considered

Watlington Station in the 1920's. *(Courtesy Mrs. Clarke & Mrs. Watts)*

necessary for its protection must, however, have been agreed, for good relations were sufficiently established for Grierson of the G.W.R. to be authorised in July of 1871 to negotiate an arrangement for working the Watlington company's line. In March the next year, a draft was submitted to the Great Western Board of an agreement to do away with the intended junction, and instead double the line from the site of the intended junction to the Risborough station. The cost was estimated at £2,500, of which the Watlington company agreed to pay £1,352 in addition to the working and maintenance cost which would have been incurred had the junction been laid, estimated at £70 p.a. The work was to proceed once the Watlington Railway paid the £1,352. June saw the authorisation by the G.W.R. of expenditure of £1,061 on the platform and sidings at Risborough required by the Board of Trade, and later the same month the Great Western seal was affixed to the junction and working agreements with the Watlington and Princes Risborough Railway.

Meanwhile, construction of the railway had been proceeding, and the line was opened throughout on August 15th 1872. The financial climate had obviously eased since the days when the Wallingford and Watlington company had been trying to raise capital for its extension across the Thames. By the end of 1872, £43,299 had been raised, of which £31,188 was share capital, £12,000 raised by loans carrying 5% interest, and the remaining £111 being interest on the funds in hand. All the capital had been subscribed as, of course, required before loans could be raised: £28 was outstanding and there had been a discount on the £36,000 authorised totalling £4,784. Of the total thus far £37,080 had been spent.

The line was cheaply made and, as has been noted, followed as far as possible the contours of the land, skirting the hills which were never far away to the southeast. The rails were 54 lbs per yard Vignolles section, fastened with dog-spikes to the sleepers which were not ballasted in the usual way, but apparently embedded in the chalk soil and filled in where required with more chalk dug from along the lineside. Although an undertaking had been given to the Board of Trade before the line opened to work it on the train staff and ticket system — which, incidentally, was first introduced on the Wycombe Railway on its opening to Thame in 1862 — this was never complied with, and the line was operated with one engine in steam from the outset. The station buildings at Watlington, Aston Rowant and Chinnor were near identical in appearance, being neat one-storied constructions in a pleasing Rustic Gothic style, well

21

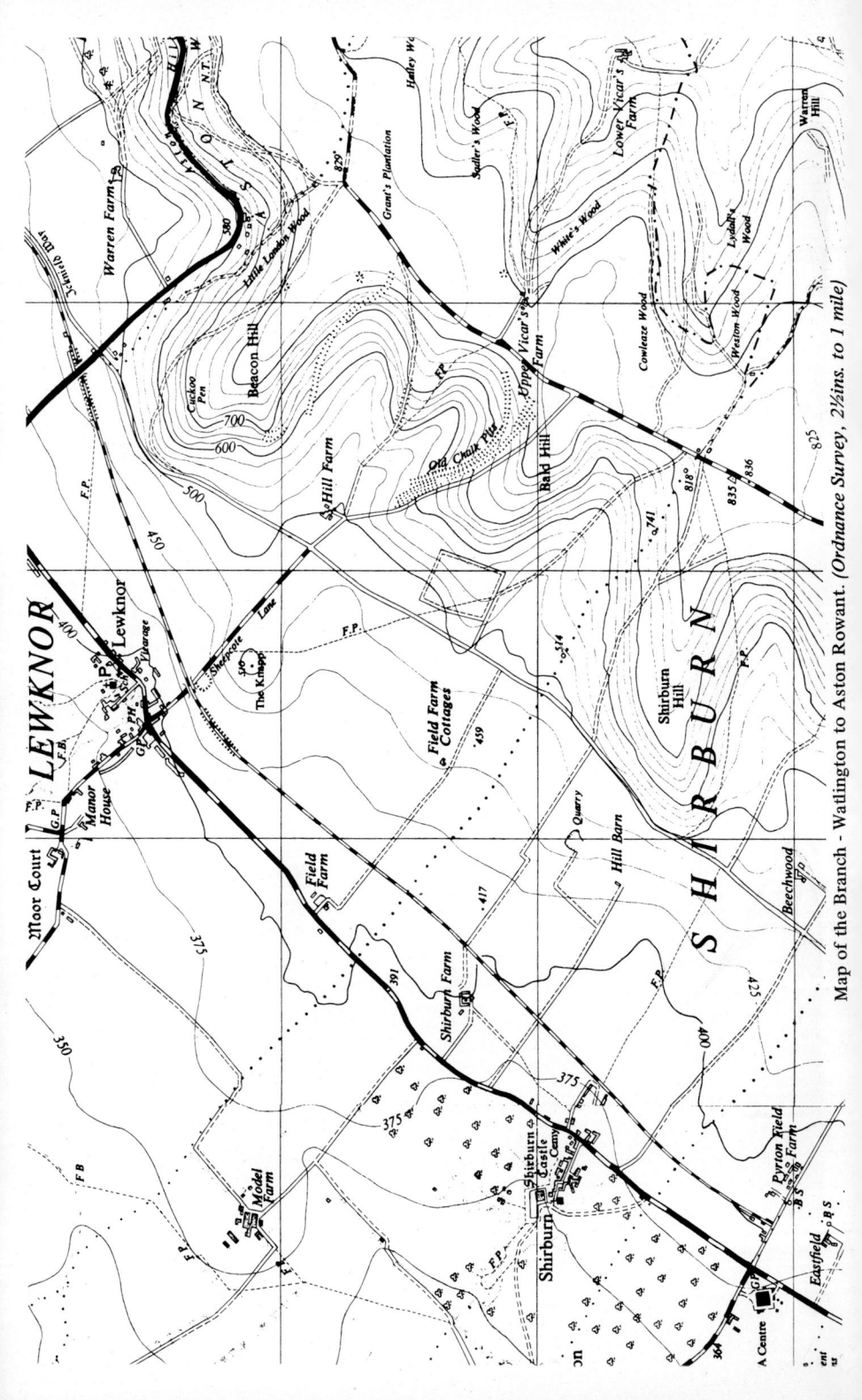

Map of the Branch - Watlington to Aston Rowant. (Ordnance Survey, 2½ins. to 1 mile)

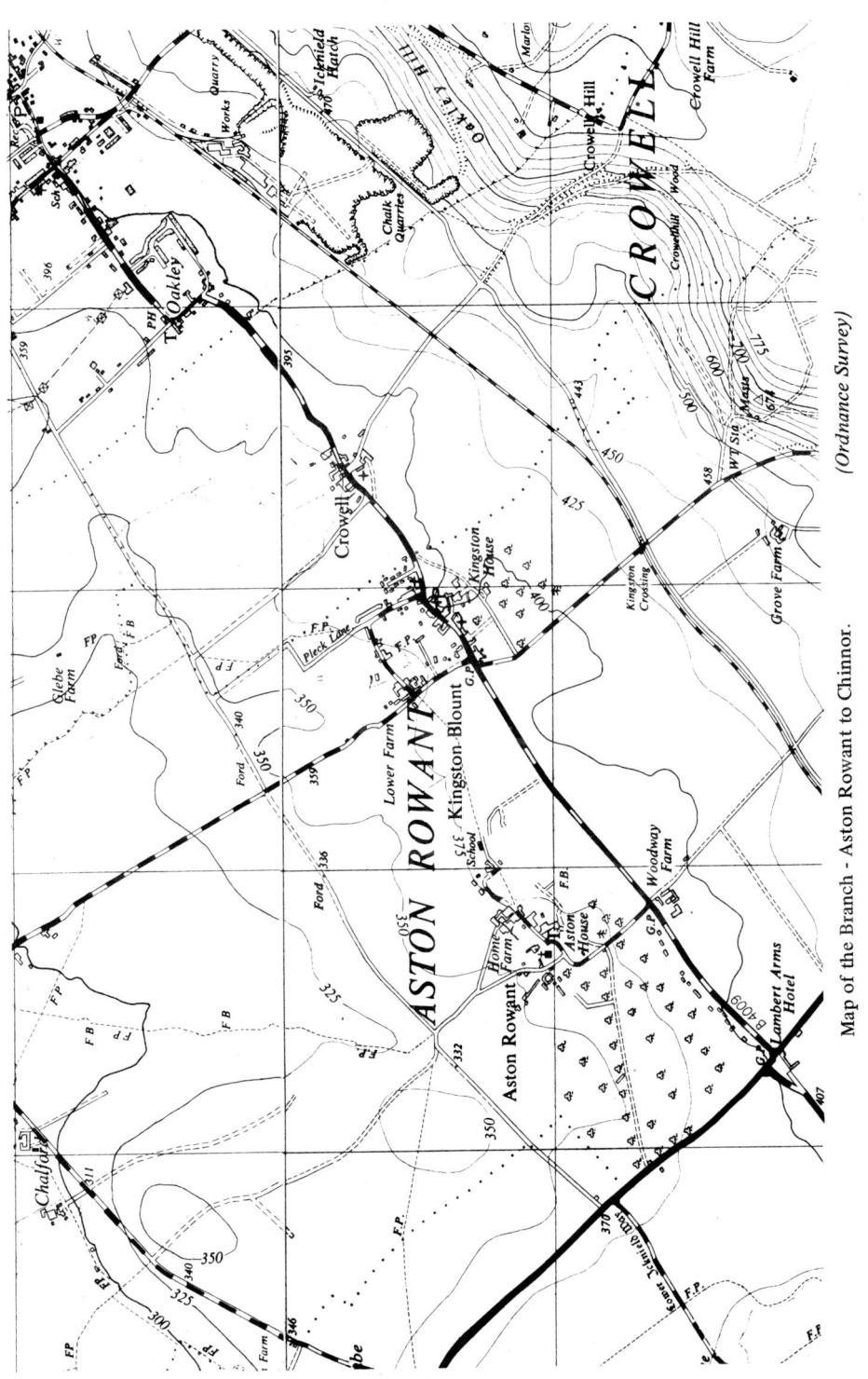

Map of the Branch - Aston Rowant to Chinnor.

(Ordnance Survey)

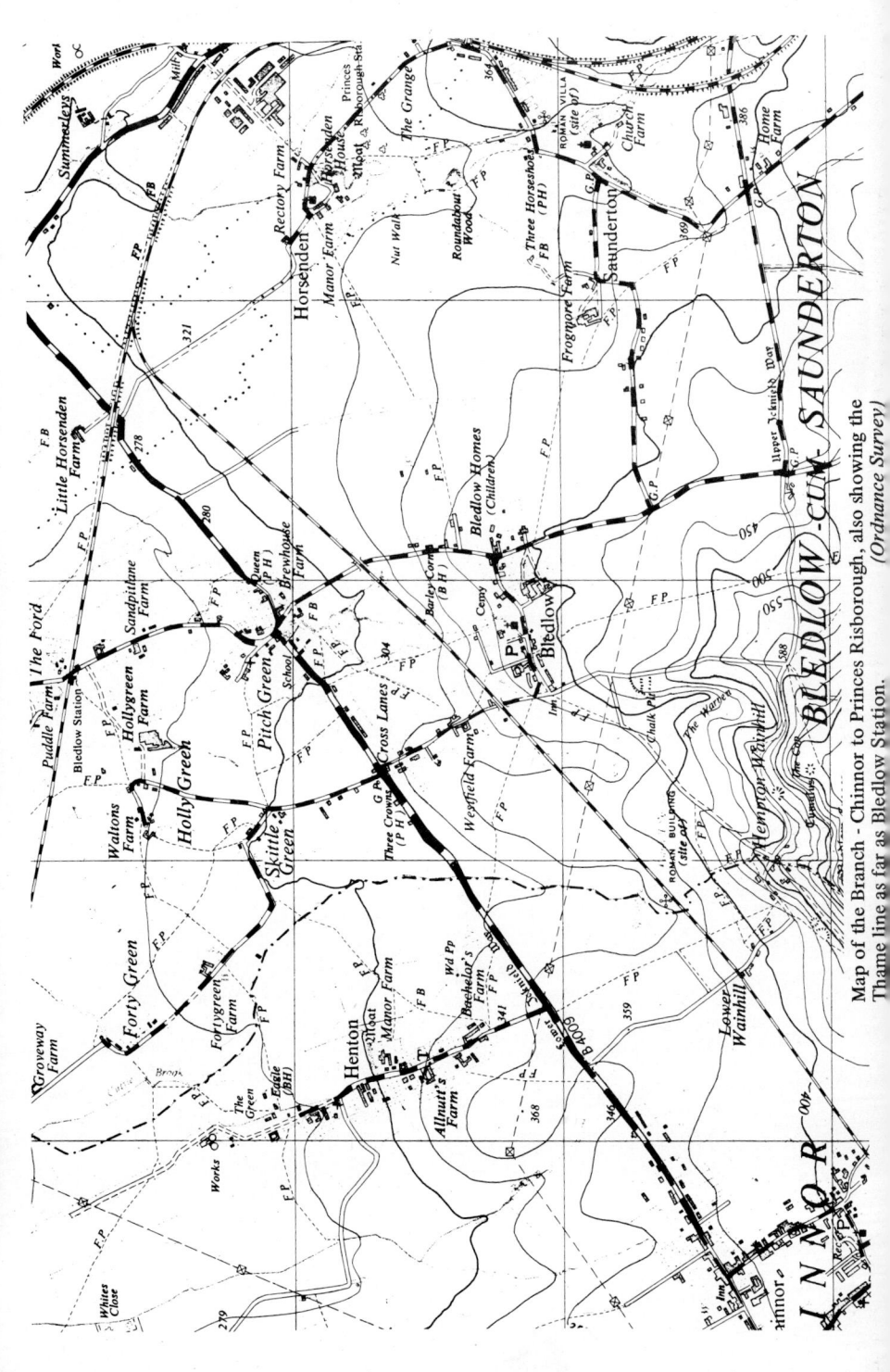

Map of the Branch - Chinnor to Princes Risborough, also showing the
Thame line as far as Bledlow Station.
(Ordnance Survey)

suited to their surroundings. At the Princes Risborough end, there appears to have been some delay in the works, and trains are believed to have terminated at a wooden platform short of the Great Western station for a while.

Regrettably, good relations with the Great Western Railway were shortlived. By the seventh general meeting, not much more than six months after the opening, it was reported that "with a view to develop the traffic, the Directors have obtained a supply of wagons and sheets on hire from the Midland Wagon Co. of Birmingham, having experienced great difficulty in getting a proper supply from the G.W. Rly. Co. for this purpose."

In February 1874, a balance of £565 was reported to the Great Western Board as outstanding against the Watlington company, in addition to the tolls for use of a portion of the Great Western of at least £150 p.a. Repeated applications had been made for payment, but without effect. In March, the figure outstanding on traffic account was about £340, and the Watlington railway was counterclaiming for losses incurred as the result of delays in carrying out the works of the junction.

On the 24th April 1875, Taylor, Chairman of the Watlington and Princes Risborough Railway, wrote to Sir Daniel Gooch at Paddington suggesting that the Great Western take a three year lease of the branch at a rent of £600 p.a., to be defrayed against the sums owing by the Watlington company, and maintaining that the line was about paying its way, which was far from true, and that traffic was increasing. The Great Western Directors authorised Mr. Grierson to negotiate. Meanwhile, matters had gone from bad to worse, and in October the outstanding balance for the hire of rolling stock, junction charges and tolls was £1,972, and the Great Western were on the brink of taking legal action. A letter at the beginning of November from the Earl of Macclesfield, who had by this time become a Director, succeeded in winning a fortnight's reprieve.

The truth was that the Watlington railway's finances were in a parlous state. Up to the end of 1875, expenditure had consistently exceeded revenue. From the opening to the end of 1872, costs had been £789 of which the largest item was £436 for the loco. power and hire of stock. Income, on the other hand, amounted to only £666 of which £390 was from goods and parcels. The accounts show 613 first class bookings, 990 second, 3,122 third and 2,064 parliamentary, contributing to the passenger receipts total. For the next half year, the deficit was £165 on receipts of £955, while the expenditure was greater than this would imply since there were outstanding liabilities carried over. A deficit of £616 was recorded for the last six months of 1873, and the Directors had dipped into their own pockets to the tune of £1,420 by the end of the year. The accounts were charged with £105 for junction expenses at Risborough due since the opening of the line, as well as the minimum tolls, but the report is vague about whether these sums had actually changed hands.

1874 saw deficits of £414 and £227 for the half years, and a reduction in goods receipts was noted as a result of the uncertain state of the coal traffic and reduction in the rates for corn and other goods. For the first half of 1875, expenditure was £1,405 against receipts of £850, while for the second half the figures were £1,310 and £1,134. The Directors had meanwhile entered into an arrangement with the 'Watlington Rolling Stock Co.' for the use of their locomotives and carriages "which they confidently hope will conduce to the more economical working of the line." The working agreement with the Great Western Railway had clearly proved burdensome.

The Watlington company scraped together a cheque for £664 in part payment in mid-November, and stated that the balance would be paid off during the ensuing year. The Great Western could scarcely be expected to regard this as satisfactory, and insisted that the W. & P.R. Rly. nominate someone to agree the actual amount due, this to be paid off by the end of January the next year, 1876. The Watlington company must nevertheless have succeeded in prevaricating further, for in the following October the sum owing was over £2,000. Of this, about £600 was for tolls over and above the minimum fixed by Act of Parliament which, not having been finally agreed, had not been debited. The Secretary of the Watlington company finally offered to pay for the future £250 p.a. in full settlement of tolls, junction and station expenses — which was very little more than the previous minimum for junction costs and running powers. In addition, the balance due from the previous 30th June, £1,173, would be paid as well as the £600 referred to.

This was still an inadequate offer for the Great Western Directors, who authorised Grierson to negotiate on the basis of immediate payment, or subsequent payment with interest, of the whole sum, and this being done, of £75 p.a. for junction expenses, £150 p.a. in lieu of tolls and £200 p.a. for station expenses. The bargaining continued. The Watlington company replied with much the same

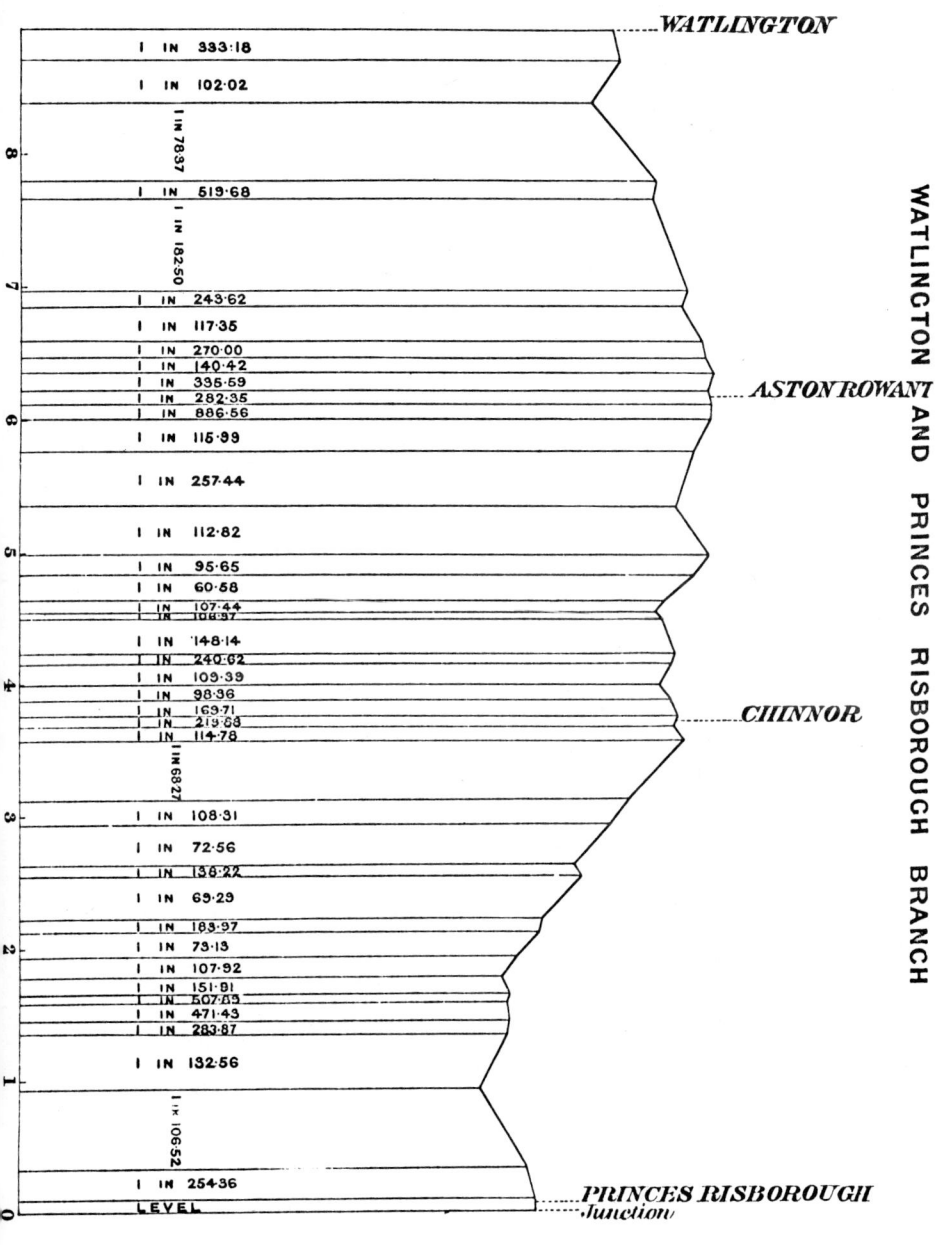

WATLINGTON

1 IN 333:18

1 IN 102·02

1 IN 78·37

1 IN 519·68

1 IN 182·50

1 IN 243·62

1 IN 117·35

1 IN 270·00
1 IN 140·42
1 IN 335·59
1 IN 282·35
1 IN 886·56

1 IN 115·99

ASTON ROWANT

1 IN 257·44

1 IN 112·82

1 IN 95·65

1 IN 60·58

1 IN 107·44
1 IN 108·57

1 IN 148·14

1 IN 240·62

1 IN 109·39

1 IN 98·36

1 IN 169·71
1 IN 219·63
1 IN 114·78

CHINNOR

1 IN 68·27

1 IN 108·31

1 IN 72·56

1 IN 136·22

1 IN 65·29

1 IN 183·97

1 IN 73·13

1 IN 107·92

1 IN 151·91
1 IN 507·65
1 IN 471·43
1 IN 283·87

1 IN 132·56

1 IN 106·52

1 IN 254·36

LEVEL

PRINCES RISBOROUGH
Junction

WATLINGTON AND PRINCES RISBOROUGH BRANCH

Gradient Profile.

(Public Record Office)

27

offer while the Great Western "in order to meet the difficulty of the Watlington company as far as possible" moderated their own demands slightly and offered to leave the matter to an arbitrator.

The Watlington and Princes Risborough, doubtless sensing that they were beginning to get the upper hand, replied that if their own previously stated proposals were not accepted, they would have to close the line. The G.W.R. therefore suggested a personal interview, and Lord Macclesfield, Mr. Taylor and Mr. Robinson, the Directors of the company at the time, duly presented themselves at Paddington in December 1876. Here, finally, agreement was reached, with the Watlington company agreeing to pay the sum of £1,173 before the year-end, and the Great Western settling for £250 p.a. in future for tolls etc. Certain minor debts were also to be paid, and the agreement was to be without prejudice to the right of either party to revert to the original agreement. The G.W.R. seal was finally affixed to the new agreement nearly a year later, in October 1877.

From this exhausting dispute with the Watlington railway's powerful neighbour, it would be well to return to the quieter scene at Watlington, or more precisely the Hare and Hounds Inn, where the Company's meetings were held. The original Directors continued in office until 1875 when F. E. S. Viret died, and the number was then reduced to three, the minimum stipulated in the Act of Incorporation. All the original Directors with the exception of Thomas Taylor, the Chairman, stood down and were replaced at the November meeting by the Earl of Macclesfield and Edward Robinson. At the same meeting, R. W. Lemmon was appointed Secretary on the retirement of C. E. Peel, who had only succeeded to the position six months earlier and was himself the third holder of the post. In contrast to this rapid turnover, Robert Lett was station master at Watlington from the opening of the line until he retired in 1900. At first sight, the requirements of three trains each way daily (excluding Sundays) would not have placed too much of a burden on operating staff, but the traffic receipts indicated no shortage of minerals, merchandise and farm produce to be handled, and all the trains were potentially mixed with both passenger vehicles and goods wagons. Train mileage, which was 6,372 for the 4½ months from opening, remained at the same level of around 8,400 miles per half year thereafter.

From the mid-1870's traffic began to increase, so that for the first half of 1878 the Directors were able to record an excess of income

Watlington, looking towards the junction, taken in June 1951 before the wooden extension of the platform originally used for milk traffic was demolished.

(R.F.G. Simpson)

The Station Forecourt at Watlington *(R.F.G. Simpson)*

Aston Rowant in the 1950's looking towards Watlington (above) and Chinnor (below). *(Lens of Sutton)*

over expenditure, albeit a modest £4. Bookings for the half year numbered 552 first class, 1,454 second, 4,949 third, and 2,477 parliamentary. The effect of pennypinching in the early years of operation was now beginning to take its toll. For the next half year, a deficit of £210 was recorded, the increase in expenditure being ascribed to an item for £233 for iron fences to prevent cattle straying onto the line. The pattern was repeated in 1879, with a small profit in the early months offset by a loss later in the year from increased expenditure on carriages and wagons due to rebuilding of the wagons. The rolling stock was by this time the property of the Railway, having been transferred from that convenient fiction, the Watlington Rolling Stock Company. The formation of a separate corporate entity, in this case the Watlington Rolling Stock Co., to buy equipment and lease it to the parent company was a well-known device, and allowed the W. & P.R. to be saved a capital outlay it could ill-afford in return for a hire charge on the revenue account.

Cumulatively over the next two years, the Railway managed to just more than break even, but internal dissatisfaction at the situation was evident from the changes on the Board. Edward Robinson retired early in 1881, and was replaced by A. H. C. Brown. The Earl of Macclesfield resigned at the end of June, followed within a year by Brown, leaving Taylor alone in the Chair with at minimum two vacancies to fill to comply with the Act of Incorporation. This was not done until December 1882 when J. H. W. Peel — one of the original Directors — and Edward Robinson were re-elected to the Board.

Doubtless they felt obliged to reassert their influence on the direction of the Company in defence of interests other than those represented by Taylor. For events had moved speedily in the meantime. In February of 1882, the Watlington company approached the Great Western to see if the agreement for use of Princes Risborough station, which had expired at the end of the previous year, could be renewed for a further five years on the same terms. The Great Western Directors authorised negotiations, and these probably prompted a further approach to the G.W.R. to absorb the line, the earlier approach having come to nothing as a result of the financial bickering between the two companies.

It was reported at a Great Western Board meeting at the beginning of November 1882 that "Mr. Taylor is desirous of this Company either working or purchasing the Watlington and Princes Risborough Railway". Taylor submitted a statement of the railway's financial position and a report from a Mr. Owen on the present condition of the line. He also stated that Mr. Toogood (who had been connected with the W. & P.R. since its promotion) "is desirous of obtaining the co-operation of this Company in an application to Parliament for powers to construct a railway from Watlington to Didcot, Wallingford or Reading." The Board declined to entertain Mr. Toogood's suggestion, but authorised the General Manager to negotiate for the acquisition of the Watlington and Princes Risborough line.

And so the seemingly endless argument and negotiation between the two companies began once more. Grierson, in mid November, reported the heads of an agreement proposed by Mr. Taylor as follows:

1. The G.W.R. to pay the Watlington company £1,500 on July 1st 1883 "to settle outstanding debts".

2. The G.W.R. to give bonds at 4% for £12,000 with interest thereon not to be payable until the beginning of 1885.

3. The G.W.R. to give bonds at 4% for £9,500, interest not to be payable until 1890.

4. Rolling stock to be purchased at a valuation.

5. The line to be properly maintained until handed over.

Taylor had apparently also suggested a further bond for £3,000 but sanction for this was declined by the Great Western Directors. In reply, Grierson accordingly prefaced his proposed terms of settlement with "it was foreseen the difficulty was to show the Watlington and Princes Risborough as it exists is of any real value inasmuch as, as it stands, it cannot pay the working expenses and the rent and payments due to this Company . . . . . and as this Co. would have to spend many thousand pounds upon the line if we took it over, the Directors were unable to agree to the terms suggested in your letter".

The proposed terms of settlement listed by Grierson were accepted by Taylor by the end of November and Taylor, who seemed to consider that the degree of his own involvement with the Railway justified the somewhat high-handed attitude he had adopted in pursuing an agreement without reference to anyone else connected with the Watlington company, was left to "sell" the terms to the Watlington shareholders. Not surprisingly, bearing in mind that total expenditure on capital account amounted to £50,433 and the proposed purchase price added up to just £24,700, the reaction at the meeting called six months later in June 1883 was hostile to say the least. The two newly-appointed Directors spoke out against the merger, and it was pointed out that Taylor had not been alone in dipping into his own pocket with loans to keep the line running!

Chinnor in the summer sunshine in post-nationalisation days, viewed (above) towards the junction and (below) towards Aston Rowant.

(Lens of Sutton)

Taylor was accordingly obliged to return to the Great Western in June and ask for modification of the agreement to which the G.W.R. seal had been fixed at the end of May. His letter stated that the Watlington shareholders were in unanimous opposition to the terms agreed. The sum to be paid was considered much below the line's value, and there was objection to the bonds being for five years only. Taylor was prepared to accept £20,000 in cash or debenture stock instead of the bonds for £21,500, but the Great Western declined to sanction any increase in the sum to be paid, although they were willing to pay cash to the present value of the bonds, estimated at £18,000.

By early July, the Watlington shareholders had agreed to the Great Western terms previously agreed with Taylor. What made them change their minds is not recorded, since there was no improvement in the offer other than an assurance that the Great Western would extend the duration of the bonds to twenty years. Perhaps they feared that if now they refused, the G.W.R. would lose interest altogether.

The Railway was accordingly vested in the Great Western on the 1st July 1883, the major Company having insisted meanwhile on inserting a clause limiting their liability to what they actually paid for the Watlington line; and the purchase was confirmed by the Great Western Railway Act of the 29th August that year. Full possession was not, however, taken until the end of the year, and the last general meeting of the Watlington company was held in mid-January 1884, when a deficit of £77 on revenue account was recorded for the first half of the previous year. The same date of 15th January also saw an extraordinary meeting of shareholders for the purpose of winding up the company and appointing a liquidator. Inevitably, Thomas Taylor was appointed to the position and soon proved as much a thorn in the side of the Great Western as Liquidator as he had as Chairman.

The problems associated with the Great Western's new acquisition were not long in coming to light. The valuation of stock, which formed part of the purchase price and amounted to £1,714, was submitted by William Dean in August 1883, and indicated that little of the rolling stock was of much use without substantial renewals. In the same month, £3,750 was authorised to put the line in proper order, prematurely it seems, since three months later Mr. Owen's report on the condition of the line became available. This was presumably a second report by Owen, the first having been submitted by Taylor a year earlier. Be that as it may, it made gloomy reading, indicating that because of decay in the sleepers and rails, expenditure of £7,010 would be necessary to maintain the line for light engines, or £9,827 if the branch was to be made fit for the ordinary rolling stock of the Great Western. A further report by a Mr. Holden described the road as "in chalk without ballast and the greater part unfenced, and in wet weather the engines must suffer severly from dirt thrown up in passing as the road is in very defective condition". Mr. Owen was authorised to put the line into a thorough state of repair at the least possible cost.

There were also difficulties over the lack of proper boundaries and conveyances for the land which the line crossed. Apparently, only receipts for the land purchased by the Watlington company were issued, saving the cost and trouble of conveyancing. This, Taylor remarked, had been at the suggestion of the solicitors, who would consequently be depriving themselves of the fees for the work! Pressed over the absence of plans for the line, Taylor stated that Messrs. Wilkinson and Smith had been engineers for the railway, but that he had had nothing to do with them since the opening. So, by implication, the Great Western had better sort it out with the engineers.

A series of increasingly acid letters from Taylor testified to protracted dispute over certain stores removed from railway premises, over payment of interest for the second half of 1883 on the £1,500 forming part of the financial settlement, and over the issue and endorsement of bonds. The Great Western offer in June 1883 to extend these to twenty years duration was not accepted by Taylor, and consequently not incorporated in the agreement. Within four months, however, Taylor changed his mind and requested extension of the term of the bonds. The Great Western Railway somewhat reluctantly agreed to this, although the correspondence dragged on some while longer.

Nor were the obstructive tactics reserved for the purchaser alone. Messrs. Adams and Co. of Manchester wrote to the Great Western late in 1884 bemoaning the fact that they had a small account outstanding against the Watlington company, but could get no reply as to who would pay it.

The Great Western was obliged to resort to withholding small outstanding sums in an attempt to prise documents from the Watlington liquidator. Thomas Taylor's letter of September 1886 was an example of the depths to which the squabbling had sunk. He wrote "as soon as £10.5.5d. due by the Great Western Co. to the liquidator of the Watlington Co. is paid, I will endeavour to procure for you the Minute book you require. The above amount is the balance of an account for stores of the Watlington Co. amounting to £67.8.4d of which you have only paid £57.2.11d." The Great Western never obtained its Minutes. Mrs. Taylor wrote in November 1891 and, referring to the ill health of her husband, indicated that the papers, which would have provided much information of subsequent historical interest, had gone to the mills as waste when the Taylors left Aston Rowant House.

Thus did the Watlington and Princes Risborough Railway sink into comparative obscurity in the Great Western empire. Its eleven year independent existence had been marked by dispute; financial difficulties — expenditure had exceeded revenue by 12% over those years — had dogged its progress.

CHAPTER III

Early Locomotives and Rolling Stock

Details of the motive power and stock used for the first three years from the opening of the line, and provided by the Great Western Railway under the working agreement, have not survived. Trains on the Great Western's own branch lines of the period were scarcely noted for their excellence, so there is no reason to suppose that anything very opulent found its way onto the Watlington line, particularly once the Watlington company proved tardy in paying the hire charges. The conviction that working the line itself would be more economical probably prompted the W. & P.R. Rly. to go it alone, but the disincentive to potential travellers afforded by the worst Great Western carriages of the time doubtless encouraged the decision. Thus in 1875, the Watlington Directors set about acquiring their own rolling stock.

The first locomotive to reach the line was a second-hand 2-2-2 well-tank which arrived in September of 1875. This had been built by Sharp Stewart, works number 1016, and was one of two sold in 1857 to the Furness Railway, on whose line it ran as No. 11. It was resold to Sharp Stewart in 1875, and was then acquired by the Watlington company at a cost of £900. The single driving wheels were 5ft. 6ins. in diameter, which can hardly have contributed to the engine's suitability for the steep gradients and slow speeds of the Watlington line. Nevertheless, it continued in service in increasing disrepair until the end of the Railway's independent existence in 1883.

The valuation of rolling stock completed in August of that year attributed little better than scrap value — £220 — to W. & P.R. No. 1, and described the engine as having a wheelbase of 14ft. 6ins., cylinders 14ins. by 18ins. stroke, boiler pressure of 120 lbs. per sq. in., water capacity of 650 gallons, and a weight of 24 tons 10 cwt. It was also described as being in working order, which was only just true. Mr. Holden's report, previously mentioned, stated of No. 1 that "it is in very defective condition, good for nothing but scrap. The copper box appears to be thin, and tube plates much eaten away. Both outside frames broken and patched . . . motion old fashioned . . leading and trailing tyres very thin".

No photographs are known to exist of this engine, either as W. & P.R. No. 1 or as Furness No. 11. An impression of its appearance can, however, be gained from the photograph of the sister engine, formerly Furness No. 12/12A, taken when running as "Clevedon" on the Weston, Clevedon and Portishead Railway, to whom it was sold by the Furness company in 1898.

The ugly cab on "Clevedon" was a later addition as, almost certainly, was the feed pipe to the side of the dome. No. 11 would have been equipped with the characteristic Sharp Stewart weatherboard extended down to the bunker front in an inverted "U", and the bunker would have had a flared top, also typical of Sharp Stewart practice of the period. The engine would not have possessed vacuum brake equipment in either Furness or W. & P.R. ownership, this and the other differences from "Clevedon" contributing to a much better proportioned and less cluttered appearance.

Coincidentally, the Weston, Clevedon and Portishead Railway subsequently purchased the second Watlington and Princes Risborough locomotive. Watlington No. 2 was also a Sharp Stewart engine, works number 2578, but purchased new in February 1876 for £1,475. It was a 2-4-0 tank engine with 2ft. 9ins. leading and 4ft. coupled wheels and thus more suited to the gradients of the line. Wheelbase was 12ft. 5ins. and the tanks held 400 gallons of water. The boiler was 9ft. 3ins. long, one foot less than on No. 1, while the firebox was 2ft. 6ins. inside compared with 3ft. 1ins. Working

"Clevedon' of the Weston, Clevedon and Portishead Railway, sister engine of Watlington and Princes Risborough Rly. No.1.

Seal of the Watlington and Princes Risborough Railway.
(Courtesy Great Western Railway Museum, Swindon)

Furness Railway 2-2-2 well tank locomotive No. 21, built in 1864. A good impression of the earlier, 1857-built, engine of this type as sold to the W. & P.R.Rly. can be gained by substituting the cab and bunker of No.21 on "Clevedon".

pressure was identical to that of No. 1 at 120 lbs., but cylinders were only 12ins. by 17ins.

At the time of purchase by the Great Western, No. 2 was in rather better condition, as befitted its more recent building date, and attracted a valuation of £850. It had, nevertheless, deteriorated to a marked extent, and was described as being badly in need of a thorough overhaul. The righthand leading and driving axle springs were broken and cramped together, while the lefthand driving wheel boss was cracked. Spokes in both driven wheels were loose in their bosses, boiler tubes were leaking, and the boiler was in very dirty condition, no doubt the result of the hard water raised from chalk ground. W. & P.R. Rly. No. 2 was surprisingly long-lived, and its subsequent history will be followed in the next chapter.

No details have survived of the paint scheme for motive power, but the list of repairs carried out on one engine by Manning Wardle at Hunslet, Leeds, included provision for repainting, lining and revarnishing.

The first three passenger carriages, including a passenger brake van, probably came to Watlington second-hand, for they were lying derelict at Chinnor in 1883, and were considered valueless except for the old metal. The composite was 17ft. 6ins. long and 7ft. 9ins. wide over mouldings, and contained one second class and two first class compartments. Height from floor to roof inside was 6ft. The other two were identical in width and height, but 19ft. long. The third class carriage contained four compartments while the brake van had one third class compartment and provision for guard and luggage. Springs were 6ft. long and wheels 3ft. in diameter except for the van, which had 3ft. 6ins. wheels.

Three new carriages were ordered from the Lancaster Wagon Company in 1878. The specification for these, dated June, indicated a composite, with two compartments each for first and second class seating respectively 16 and 20 passengers, a third class carriage with accommodation for 50 in five compartments, and a brake van, all to be delivered free on the Watlington and Princes Risborough within four months of June 4th at a cost of £800.

The carriages were quite well appointed by the standards of the day. The first class had blue cloth and morocco, trimmed with lace, sprung seats and backs, and carpet on the floor. The roof and sides above the squabs were covered in ornamental wax cloth with gilt mouldings and, as well as the customary hat cords, there were luggage racks of the net variety with ornamental brackets and rods.

Doors had vertically sliding windows with sliding ventilators above, while the sidelights were provided with Merino curtains which extended to meet in the middle over the doorlights. The second class compartments were upholstered in blue worsted with seats and backs of stuffed horsehair. The umbrella racks and hat cords of the first class were repeated in the second class, and doors again had sliding windows, but there were no blinds and no carpet on the floor, and woodwork, where not upholstered, was stained imitation teak and varnished. The third class was, of course, more spartan. Doors had sliding windows, but ventilators were fixed. The interior woodwork of seats, sides and partitions was stained teak colour and varnished, while the roof inside was painted white.

The guard was provided with a 6ft. compartment with side lookouts called a caboose in the specification, containing seat lockers, shelves, and a screw brake with one brake block acting on each of the four wheels. There was also a luggage compartment reached by folding doors. All three carriages had spoked wheels, 3ft. 6ins. in diameter, with Mansell's patent retaining rings securing the tyres. Buffers, 1ft. 9ins. long, and drawgear operated against laminated springs, and screw couplings were fitted.

Carriage exteriors, which had panels and mouldings in teak, were highly varnished and picked out and lettered in gold. The underframes of pitch pine, flitchplates, and headstocks of oak were painted and grained imitation teak. Ironwork, wheels, axles and springs were black with certain parts bronzed, and the roofs were covered in waterproof navy canvas and painted white lead. The 1883 report on the line described the interiors as being cased in deal; the specification had more grandiloquently called it baltic redwood. The report also indicated that the carriages had suffered severely from exposure to the weather, but were otherwise in fair condition despite a profusion of split panels attributed to construction from inadequately seasoned timber. Stripping, re-priming and painting or varnishing were recommended. The composite and third class carriages had continuous footboards, but one on the composite had been broken some time previous to 1883 and never replaced. It was, however, on the side which was not used! The van would have doubled up as a goods brake van, but the brake was inoperative at the time the Great Western took over, so woe betide any animal which strayed on the line in front of a train which had only the engine brake to hold it!

One first and second class compartment in the composite were smoking, indicated in etched letters in the sidelights. One end

No. 1384, formerly Watlington and Princes Risborough Railway No. 2, as rebuilt by the Great Western in 1899 and photographed shortly after.

(British Railways)

Another view of No. 1384, posed here with a branch passenger train, probably at Swindon and just prior to the opening of the Wrington Vale line in December 1901. No. 1384 worked on this line for the first few months of its existence.
(British Railways)

compartment in the third was for smokers, and this was separated from the others by a full height partition. The remaining four compartments were divided by one full height partition and two low ones 3ft. 4ins. from the floor, the commonly occurring economy on oil lamps being made with two only directly above the full partitions and shining, if that is the correct word, to both sides. The composite was more properly equipped with one lamp per compartment. The guard's compartment had a lamp, but there was nothing to aid porters and passengers searching for their parcels in the baggage compartment after nightfall.

To conclude on the carriages, the dimensions of the 1878 vehicles are summarised below.

	Composite	Third	Brake
Length over mouldings	26ft. 1ins.	26ft. 1ins.	20ft. 1ins.
Width over body	8ft.	8ft.	7ft. 6ins.
Width over lookouts			9ft.
Width over stepboards	9ft.	9ft.	
Width over lower steps	8ft. 4ins.	8ft. 4ins.	Not quoted.
Height inside	6ft. 8ins.	6ft. 8ins.	6ft. 8ins.
Wheelbase	15ft.	15ft.	10ft.
Length of Springs	7ft.	7ft.	7ft.

A carriage shed was provided at Watlington, and from the 1883 description this was the same structure that survives today. It was 89ft. long, 13ft. wide and 15ft. 4ins. from rail to centre of the curved roof, and covered in corrugated iron which also extended down the sides to 6ft. 4ins. from the rails.

The Company possessed six wagons, all open, and of 6 tons capacity with dumb buffers, 3ft. wheels, springs 3ft. 3ins. long, and a single brake to one wheel of each. They were purchased new on deferred payment for £59 apiece, but this excluded some of the ironwork which appears to have been second-hand: the wheels, for example, mostly dated from 1858. Nos. 1 to 3 at least were rebuilt in 1879, but much of the old ironwork was retained. Although all but No. 2 came from the Midland Wagon Co., there were some minor differences between the six, and these will be apparent from the table of dimensions.

Length inside	14ft. 1ins.
Width inside	6ft. 9ins.

Height inside	2ft. 4ins.	(No. 1)
	1ft. 9ins.	(Nos. 2 to 6)
Body	3ins. deal	
Solebars & Headstocks	1ft. by 4½ ins.	
	pitch pine	(Nos. 1 to 3)
	oak	(Nos. 4 to 6)
Wheelbase	8ft. 6ins.	(Nos. 1 to 3)
	8ft. 8ins.	(Nos. 4 to 6)

At the time of the 1883 inspection, Nos. 1 and 2 were at Watlington, Nos. 4 and 6 stopped at Chinnor with bulging tyres, and the remaining two away from their home Railway. This does not, of course, imply that there were only two wagons available on the line at that time for the carriage of goods and minerals, since the inspector would have taken no note of other railway companies' or private owner wagons present.

The Government returns unfortunately introduce an element of uncertainty into this account of the Watlington railway's rolling stock, for they first note a locomotive owned by the Company in 1874, and two in 1875, whereas we have seen that No. 1 was purchased in 1875, and only joined by the second engine the next year. It may well be, therefore, that a further locomotive was owned or hired by the Company for two years until replaced by the 2-4-0 tank engine described. The returns also cite the increase in the number of carriages from three to six as taking place in 1880. This, if correct, would indicate that the Lancaster Wagon Co. was substantially late in delivering the new vehicles despite their promise to complete the order in the Autumn of 1878. Perhaps the manufacturers were reluctant to part with the carriages until they could be sure of payment!

There are the inevitable tales of passengers in pre-Great Western Railway days having to disembark to help push the train up the steep gradients. With the lack of engine maintenance and the hard, chalky water which could soon reduce the steaming capabilities of boilers, these stories may well be believed. In 1881, the line was blocked by a severe snow-storm, and an engine and carriages became lodged for several days at a point known then as Fairy Furlong! It took all the energies of the General Manager, the Watlington Stationmaster, and a gang of labourers to dislodge the train.

CHAPTER IV

The Great Western Period

The Great Western did not set about improving its new acquisition with any great vigour, although W. & P.R. No. 1 was soon consigned to the scrapheap: the engine does not appear in the G.W.R. stock lists for 1884 and was not given a G.W.R. number. No. 2 was taken into Great Western stock and allocated the number 1384 in the 13xx series commonly reserved for absorbed engines. It must, however, have been drafted away from the Watlington branch, for it did no mileage in service down to August 1885 when work was done on the boiler. Its 108 two-inch brass tubes were then replaced by the same number of second-hand iron ones, rendering No. 1384 fit for use during the following year on the construction of the Bodmin branch.

In July 1893 when the engine had completed 74,000 miles in Great Western ownership, steam brake and apparatus for automatic vacuum brake were fitted, and boiler tubes were replaced for the third time since the 1885 repairs. It then ran for five years before tube replacements were once more called for. The former Watlington engine was by this time on loan to the Lambourn Valley Railway, on which line it operated the opening train in April 1898 and the regular service thereafter until the arrival of the L.V.R.'s own locomotives in October. No. 1384's boiler must have been deemed not worth further repair, for it was condemned in January 1899 when the engine had completed 122,000 miles with the Great Western, and replaced by one of Swindon manufacture. The main differences were a Belpaire firebox, an increase in working pressure to 150 lbs. per sq. in., and in the number of tubes, to 134. The opportunity was also taken to increase tank capacity to 638 gallons.

No. 1384 was then drafted to various lightly-laid Great Western branches, including the Wrington for part of 1901-2 and Culm Valley during parts of 1906 and 1909-10, returning on hire to Lambourn for part of 1903-4. Over the period from 1902 until April 1911 when the engine was sold to the Bute Works Supply Co., its shed allocations were to Swindon, Bristol, Severn Tunnel Junction and Exeter, as well as to Yatton, Hemyock and Lambourn for service on the three branch lines mentioned.

The Bute Works Co. quickly resold the ex-Watlington engine to the Weston, Clevedon and Portishead Railway, on whose line it became No. 4 and was named, perhaps appropriately, "Hesperus". It was finally scrapped in 1937.

Possibly the most momentous occurrence in early Great Western days was the destruction of the Watlington engine shed, which was blown down in a high wind. The two sons of the stationmaster, Mr. Lett, were inside at the time and narrowly escaped serious injury. The engine shed would seem to have had a chequered career, since its replacement was burned down in 1906 reputedly also damaging an engine within. It is scarcely surprising that providence was not tempted a third time, and the branch engine stood thereafter in the open.

Otherwise few changes were evident. The staff of the Watlington company were taken into Great Western employment and R.W. Lemmon, Secretary and General Manager of the W. & P.R. was placed on the Great Western's register of clerks. The service of three mixed trains each way on weekdays remained unchanged until after 1890, in which year the Great Western was released by the Board of Trade from the commitment to work the line by train staff and ticket. This commitment, it will be recalled, was made by the Watlington company but never adhered to. The G.W.R. thereby saved the cost of block telegraph for the branch, then estimated at £355, and one engine in steam remained the mode of operation. Such improvements as were evident certainly failed to match up to the expectations of a Lewknor farmer, Mr. Neighbour, who optimistically requested the new owners of the railway to supplement their fence with wire netting to a height sufficient to prevent turkeys and ducks flying over onto the line!

The junction arrangements altered considerably around the turn of the century as an immediate result of the development of the short cut to Birmingham. The direct line from Old Oak Common to Wycombe and from Princes Risborough to Aynho Junction was authorised under the Great Western (Additional Powers) Act of 1897, and the portion between Northolt Junction and Ashendon Junction vested in the Great Western and Great Central Joint Committee by Act of 1899. As well as these new lines and the connections for the Great Central Railway with their "old" route into Marylebone via the Metropolitan Railway, substantial improvements had to be made to the ex-Wycombe Railway section between Wycombe and Risborough, at a cost of £117,000, to bring it up to main line standards. The new route was opened for Great Central goods trains on November 20th 1905 and for passenger operation in the following April, but was not opened throughout to Aynho Junction for the use of the Great Western until the 4th April and 1st July 1910 respectively.

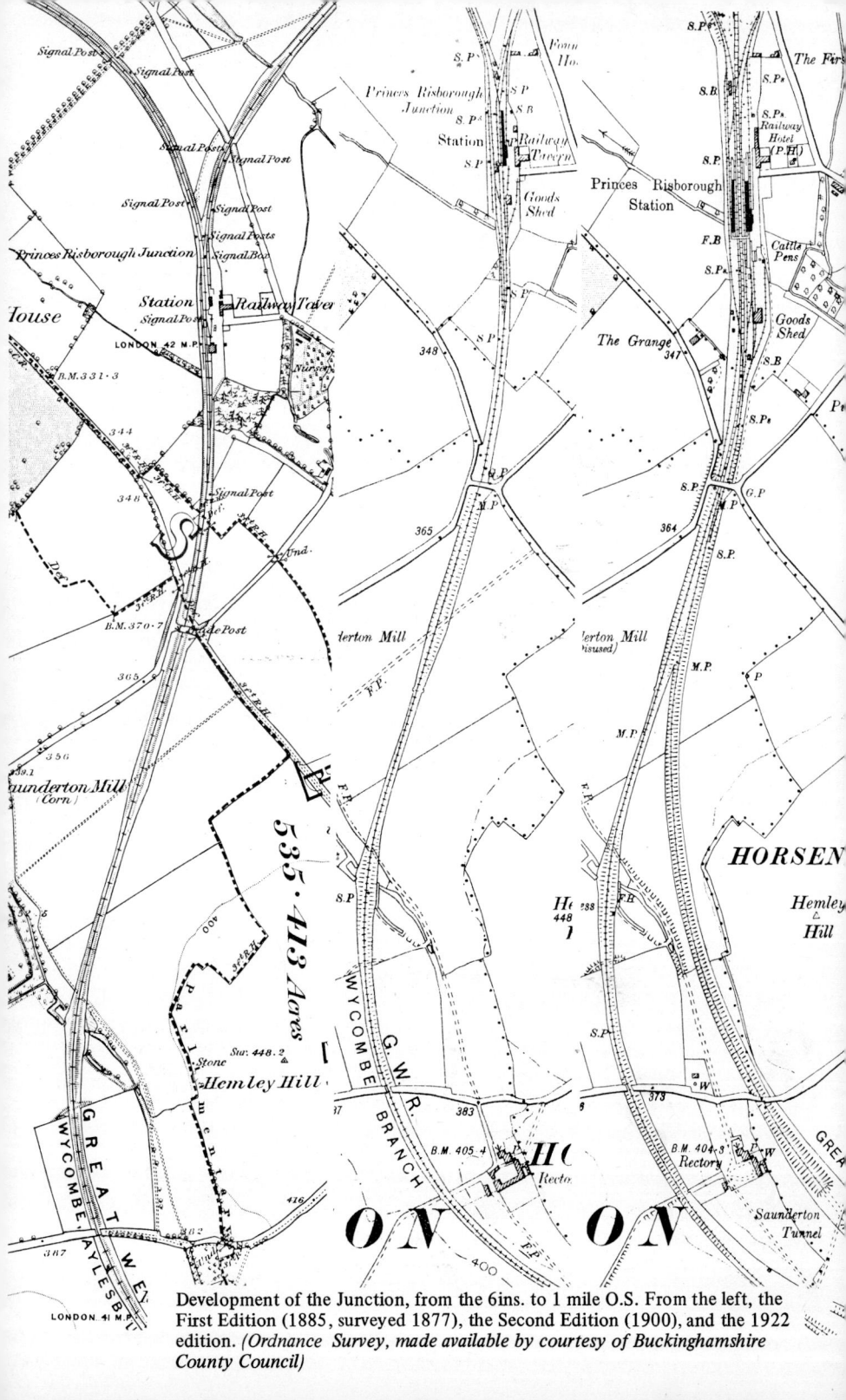

Development of the Junction, from the 6ins. to 1 mile O.S. From the left, the First Edition (1885, surveyed 1877), the Second Edition (1900), and the 1922 edition. (*Ordnance Survey, made available by courtesy of Buckinghamshire County Council*)

To accommodate the new line to the north, the old station at Princes Risborough was swept away, along with the wooden platforms and buildings serving the Watlington branch. A new station was built with two fast lines through the centre, and two main platforms facing onto loops either side. At the north end of the new station there was a bay on the up side for Aylesbury branch trains and another on the down side serving the Watlington and Thame lines. A series of scissor crossovers gave access to these branches from either platform or through roads. The goods yard remained on the up side at the south end of the station, and this could be reached from the Watlington or Thame lines by a relief road behind the down platform and bay, and a long crossover traversing all four running lines. The down side of the station, including the Watlington bay, thus became an island platform, connected by a covered footbridge with the up platform where the main offices and entrance were located.

In September 1906, three halts were opened on the Watlington branch. The first was at Bledlow Bridge, 1m. 52ch. from Princes Risborough station according to the timetable. This, as its name suggests, was sited by the bridge over a road leading to the village of that name. The halt was on the up side of the line in common with platforms at the three original stations, which were supposedly arranged that way to allow a second line of rails to be laid in easily, should this have been necessary at some later date. The schematic station plans, which show the halt as being on the down side, are incorrect in this respect.

Bledlow Bridge was equipped with a low-level platform, a hut to provide some shelter since the halt's position was very exposed, and oil lamps and nameboard. The approach was by a flight of steps alongside the bridge abutment. The railway at this point was still some distance from the village of Bledlow, but it was very much more convenient than Bledlow station on the Thame line, which was about a mile further away.

The second halt was named Kingston Crossing, sited 5m. 17ch. from Princes Risborough and half a mile from Kingston Blount on the road running southeast from that village. Another low platform was built, diagonally opposite the crossing-keeper's house and adjacent to the Icknield Way. The story is told of the owner of an Arab mare who, around 1910, challenged the train driver to a race to Chinnor from the halt. Riding along the Icknield Way, which was never more than a quarter of a mile from the railway between the two stops, he was able to beat the train.

Bledlow Bridge Halt in its declining years. The upper view is north-east towards
the junction; the lower, towards Chinnor, with the slope of the Chilterns
evident in the distance to the south. *(Lens of Sutton)*

Kingston Crossing Halt showing clear signs of impending closure, with pannier tank No. 4650 approaching with a train from Chinnor. The Icknield Way runs immediately beyond the first hedge. *(Gregory)*

Kingston Crossing looking towards Aston Rowant. The gatekeeper's house, in common with that at Wainhill, shows affinities in the design of windows and other details with the stations on the line. *(Gregory)*

The last of the halts opened in 1906 was named Lewknor Bridge and was 7m. 4ch. from the junction station. Rather unusually for the Watlington branch, it was very close to the village of Lewknor. The halt was immediately to the Watlington side of a bridge over a minor road into Lewknor at a point where the line curved sharply to the south and into a cutting. The rail-level platform with its accompanying shelter was on the down side and approached by steps from the road below.

Lewknor Bridge Halt was administered from Watlington; Kingston Blount, Bledlow Bridge and the later halt at Wainhill came under Chinnor. Stationmasters at these two stations were required to visit these unstaffed halts from time to time to see that all was in order, but during the winter months, a porter had in any case to go there every evening to instal and light the oil lamps, and every morning to remove them. Passengers boarding at halts were issued tickets on the trains. For journeys through onto the main line, fares from Aston Rowant applied to Lewknor Bridge, from Chinnor for Kingston Crossing, and from Princes Risborough for journeys commenced at Bledlow Bridge.

In 1908 Mr. W. E. Benton founded a business to manufacture lime on a 200 acre site at Chinnor, thereby creating a major source of revenue for the railway and generating the traffic which keeps the line open as far as Chinnor today. Chalk was excavated from pits opened up between the railway and the slopes of the Chilterns to the southeast, but coal to fuel the lime kilns had to be brought in by rail. In April 1910, the Great Western Directors authorised expenditure of £803 to provide a siding for the works and improve the station sidings, a further provision of £530 being made two and a half years later for more siding accommodation. The kilns, which can be seen in the aerial photograph, were set back from the railway and the sidings curved south towards them. Ultimately, there were four kilns, one of which still remains as an interesting relic.

The authorised staff establishment at Watlington in 1922 was a total of seven, made up of a stationmaster, clerk, porter, two goods porters and two passenger guards. From about 1903 to 1910, the stationmaster was a Mr. Sexton, who subsequently went to Henley. He was succeeded by Mr. Yates and from 1924 by Mr. Pocock, who appears in the centre front row in the station group taken that year, and who held the post at Watlington until 1946. From Mr. Pocock's time, the position of stationmaster at Aston Rowant was abolished, and he was responsible for that station and the intervening halt at Lewknor as well.

(Loco. & General Railway Photographs)

Change and changelessness at Lewknor Bridge Halt. Only the fashions and the generally spruce appearance betray that the upper picture antedates the lower mid-1950's view by about thirty five years. *(Lens of Sutton)*

A station group photographed at Watlington in 1924. *(Courtesy H. Humphries)*

"Hesperus" of the Weston, Clevedon and Portishead Railway, formerly Watlington and Princes Risborough Railway No. 2 and G.W.R. No. 1384. *(S.W. Baker)*

On his right in the photograph is the clerk, Miss Siarey, whose father raced the train from Kingston to Chinnor on horseback. On her right is Jimmy Nelms who was a guard on the line from about 1905 and whose father preceded him from around 1885. Finally on that side of the front row is Charlie Hopkins who started work as a porter in 1914 and retired after twenty years at Watlington and twenty-one at Aston Rowant. The attractive gardens at these two stations were largely his work. The other station staff in the photograph are "Nobby" Clarke and Harold Blackwell in the front row, and George Baker standing between the two drivers, Harry Humphries on his right and "Bumper" Jones.

Also included in the station group in addition to the locomotive firemen were the permanent way gang based at Watlington. They were responsible for the first four miles of the line from Watlington, the remainder being under the auspices of a gang working from Chinnor. Before 1938, however, the Watlington-based men were disestablished and the whole branch then came under the one permanent way gang with home station at Chinnor. The Sectional Appendix of that year authorised autotrailers to pick up or set down the men provided the site of work was at least ¼ of a mile from a station or halt!

At Aston Rowant, there was in 1922 a stationmaster and two porters and a gatewoman employed full time at Kingston Crossing. The Chinnor establishment was similar, the gatewoman in this case being responsible for Wainhill Crossing. There was, however, an additional junior porter to help with the heavier burden of traffic at Chinnor. By way of contrast, Princes Risborough had a staff of twenty-five at that date, including six signalmen to work on shift at the north and south boxes: the signal box at Watlington and ground frames elsewhere on the line were operated by whichever member of the station staff was free at the time.

Around the turn of the century, stationmasters on the branch received between £1 and £1.10s. a week according to seniority. Porters were being paid between 15s. and £1 and junior porters about half that, with the branch guards in a range between porters and stationmasters.

In September 1925, a fourth halt was brought into use at a point 2m. 75ch. from Princes Risborough and on the up side of the line. This was named Wainhill Crossing, pronounced and frequently spelt Wyn Hill, and was located immediately to the Chinnor side of the level crossing. Once again a rail level platform and shelter were

A station group posed at Watlington about 1930. The front row includes, from the left, Driver Harry Humphries, Charlie Hopkins, Stationmaster R.H. Pocock, and on the right, Driver Jeff Pearson. Standing, from the left, are Harold Blackwell, Jimmy Nelms, and on the right George Baker. To the two gentlemen whom I have been unable to identify with certainty I apologise. *(Courtesy Mrs. Clarke & Mrs. Watts)*

Wainhill Crossing Halt in the mid-1950's looking towards Chinnor (above), and Bledlow Bridge (below) with gatekeeper's house on right. *(Lens of Sutton)*

provided, although there could never have been many passengers using the halt since there were only a few houses at either Lower or Hempton Wainhill.

This was, of course, a recurring problem along the whole branch as a number of the stops were poorly located for the villages they purported to serve, and the villages themselves had only small and declining populations. A lengthy walk to the station was not of itself very much of a disincentive to travel by train in the years before car-ownership became commonplace, but declining population could scarcely help passenger services to pay their way. Aston Rowant and Kingston Blount dropped steadily from 840 residents in 1871, the year before the railway opened, to 496 in 1951. Chinnor's population fell from 1,379 in 1871 to less than a thousand, before changes in the boundaries made direct comparison impossible. At Watlington the figure was 1,943 in 1871 and 20% lower in 1911, after which the population stabilised.

Doubtless the Great Western had this type of consideration very much in mind when it reported on its branch lines in 1926 with a view to effecting economies. For the Watlington branch, the report indicated a total wage bill for the preceding year of £1,947, some 7½ percent of the traffic receipts which comprised £3,200 from passenger traffic, £4,000 from parcels and £18,400 from goods. Locomotive and train running expenses, with coal consumption at 31 lbs./mile came to 17d. per mile for passenger and nearly 19d. per mile for goods workings, giving totals of £2,900 for passenger and £1,800 for goods trains, and together 18% of receipts.

The report also recorded a daily average of seventeen coal and mineral wagons received and five forwarded, the latter of course being from the Chinnor works. On average, eight wagons carrying general goods were received daily and fifteen forwarded, and in 1925 just over 29,000 milk churns and 150 trucks of livestock were conveyed. So far as specific economies were concerned, the report recommended nothing more than the recovery of signals and signalling equipment at Watlington to give a saving worth £8 a year! This was carried out in 1929 and the signal box at Watlington was then used only for operation of points and facing point locks.

Watlington station changed little, apart from the removal of signals and the substitution of electric light at about the same date, from the time the engine shed was destroyed until closure. The arrangement of the station in the 1920's can be seen from the map, the very short loop, barely 150ft. clear between points, being a noteworthy feature. Of the three sidings, the long "back" siding was used mainly for coal trucks, the middle one was naturally required for wagons which were to be loaded or unloaded in the goods shed and the third, when not occupied by cattle trucks alongside the cattle dock, was utilised for wagons which were wanted out of the way. Milk was loaded from a timber extension at the Watlington end of the passenger platform which was built during Mr. Pocock's tenure of office.

The coal stage for locomotive purposes was located by the loop on the far side between the points giving access to engine and carriage sidings. The branch engine stood overnight over the pit on the engine siding, beyond which was a well and after 1935, the electric pumping equipment to lift water to the tower opposite. There was also a hut for permanent way stores beyond the well. The carriage shed, painted in the Great Western's stone colour, contained raised staging for the use of carriage cleaners. This operation was carried out on alternate Sundays by Watlington staff and by staff from further up the branch. In later years the substitution of a more modern autotrailer which was too wide to go between the staging meant that the carriage had to be attended to from the station platform, with ladders and planks used on the other side. Even the older trailer, however, was more often than not left out in the open overnight, it being generally considered "too much trouble" to shunt it into the shed.

Watlington station was 8m. 75ch. from Princes Risborough and almost exactly 51 miles from Paddington by the old route; it was also a goodly distance from the town of Watlington itself. The station's situation is perhaps most aptly summarised by a story recounted by the late Mr. Pocock, of the commercial traveller who alighted from the train and looked in vain for the town. Having established its direction from a farmer's lad, he asked incredulously why the station was built where it was, to which he received the reply, "Well Sir, I s'pose so that it should be near the railway".

A horse-drawn bus was operated by a Mr. Dick Smith for the landlord of the Hare and Hounds, between the station and the Hare and Hounds, an arrangement which doubtless benefited the trade at that hostelry. The horse vehicle carried six passengers, three a side, at a fare of 6d., and by the 1920's had been replaced by a Ford motor-bus of similar capacity. Dick Smith also held the agency for the delivery of parcels from the station until 1936 when it was terminated and the bus service ceased. Subsequently the

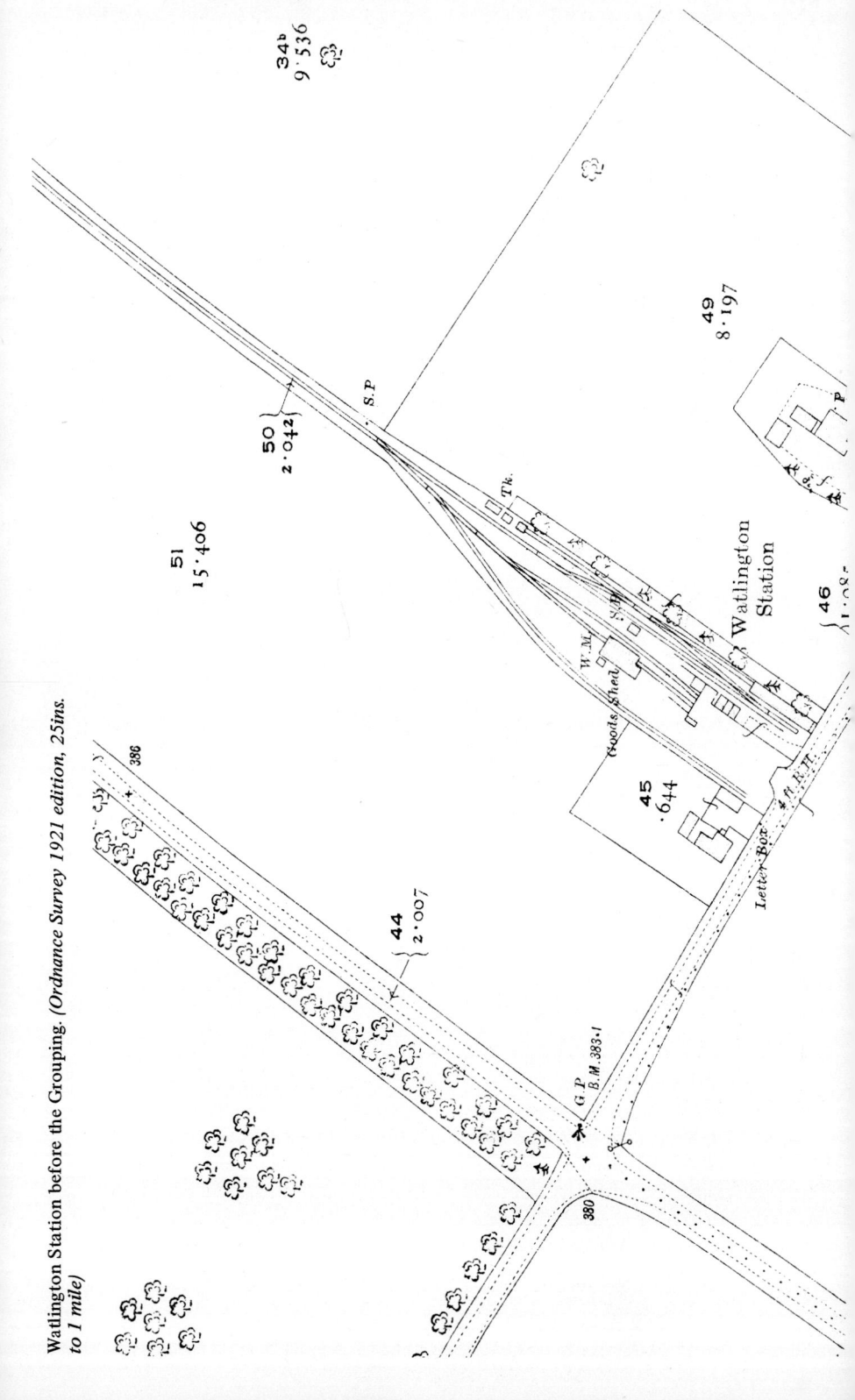

Watlington Station before the Grouping. (*Ordnance Survey 1921 edition, 25ins. to 1 mile*)

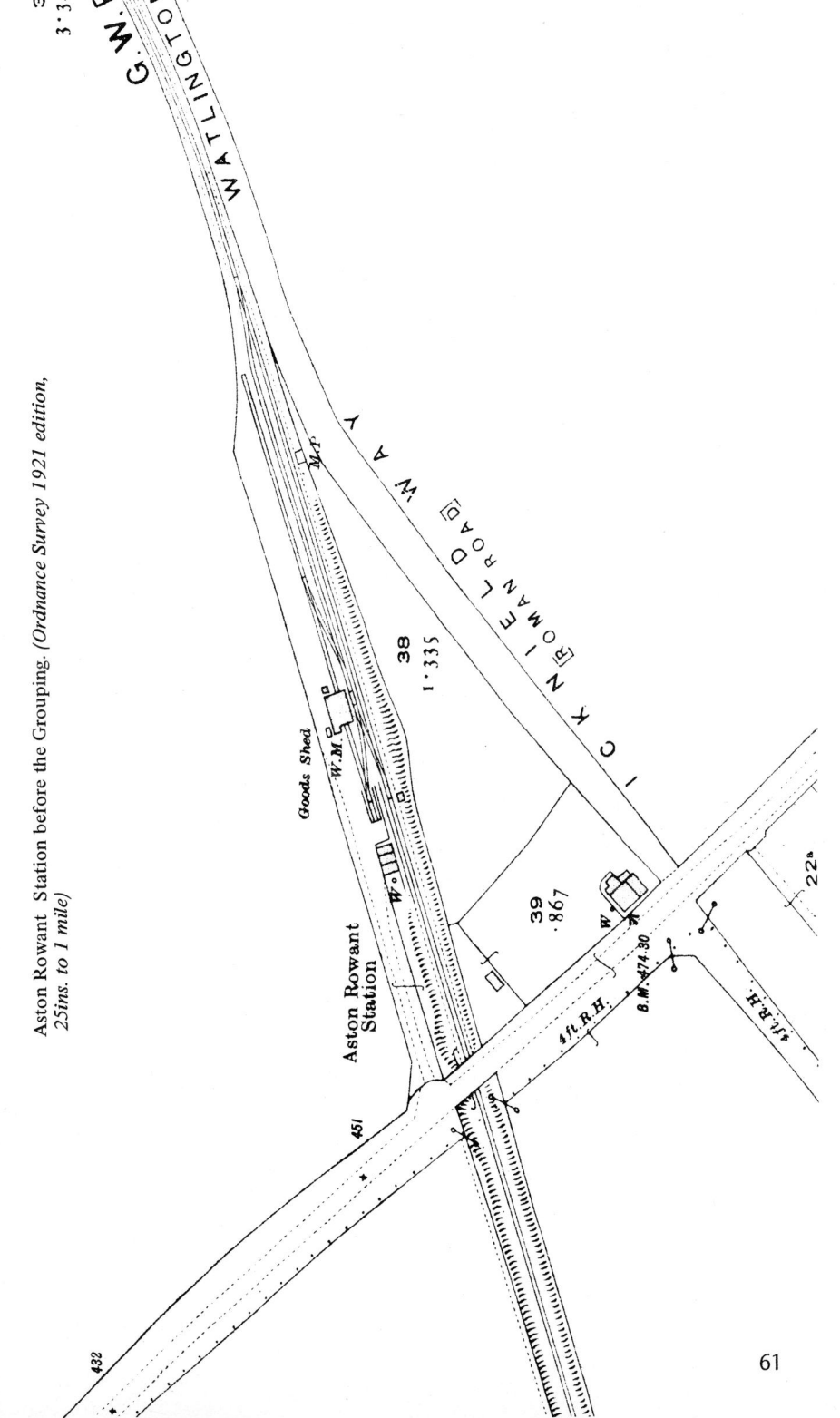

Aston Rowant Station before the Grouping. *(Ordnance Survey 1921 edition, 25ins. to 1 mile)*

61

coalmerchants, Tappin & Sons, delivered parcels until British Railways took over the task with a van based at Wallingford.

Aston Rowant station was approached by a short track from the Oxford Road, which crossed the railway by a girder bridge towards the end of the road's long descent from Aston Hill. This bridge was reconstructed and widened in 1926 at a cost of £3,000, of which the Great Western paid £1,000 and Oxfordshire County Council the remainder. The runround loop, with points at the platform end operated from a ground frame opposite the platform slope, was three times the length of that at Watlington, but against this, the station was singularly ill-equipped with siding space. The goods shed, almost identical to that at Watlington, was located on a second and very short loop off the first, the head of the loop at the station end forming a loading dock for cattle, horses, and much else, but capable of holding no more than one wagon clear of the point blades. The only reasonable length of siding was beyond the goods shed loop at the junction end of the station. But this had to be used as a headshunt for movements in and out of the shed, so its effective capacity was much reduced.

The station was 6m. 16ch. from Princes Risborough according to the timetables, but the platform was no more than 8 chains beyond the six mile post, and there is other evidence to suggest that the Great Western authorities were unsure as to the point from which they should measure distances down the branch. Aston Rowant was probably the most picturesque station on the branch with its rambling roses and tranquil air, and must come close to many people's ideal of a truly rural railway setting. It is not surprising to find that the location was used for scenes in a number of films made in the post-war period.

By contrast, Chinnor station with its background of industry and smoking chimneys presented a very different impression, although the station was in many ways similar to Aston Rowant only 2½ miles away. The map, which dates from around 1920, shows a station layout different in one or two respects from that operated in later years and, of course, substantially different from the track plan in existence to-day. The major change in the Great Western period was the substitution of direct access to the loading bay from the loop via a double slip point, instead of the access from a headshunt shown on the map. The headshunt was then connected into the other end of the slip point to provide additional siding accommodation. Throughout the period there was also a short siding branching from the Watlington end of the loop, which was of much the same length

Chinnor Station and Kilns. *(Ordnance Survey 1921 Edition)*

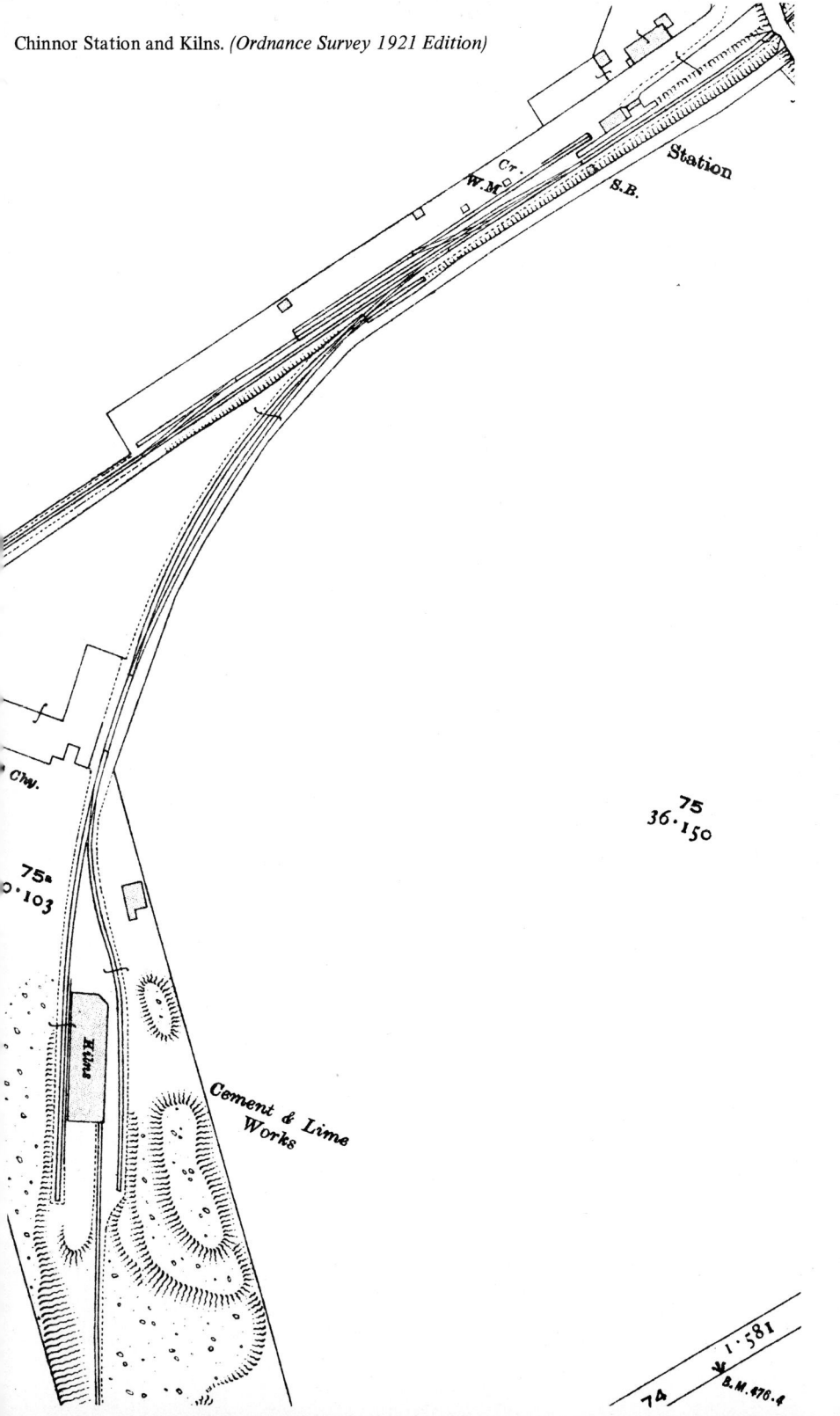

as the loop at Aston Rowant. Chinnor once possessed a goods shed similar to those at the other two stations on the line, but this would seem to have been destroyed or dismantled comparatively early in Great Western ownership.

The second world war brought about few changes on the branch other than an increase in traffic, which was handled without augmenting the existing facilities. The war did, however, bring in its wake a new economic environment in which higher wages and the door-to-door convenience of road transport had an adverse effect on the precarious financial balance of the Watlington branch and many similar lines. These developments will be considered in the final chapter.

Pannier tank and well-patronised autotrailer at Chinnor, with the cement works as background. The one remaining kiln can be seen at the far left of the picture. *(Lens of Sutton)*

BLEDLOW BRIDGE HALT
1ᴹ 43ᶜ

FROM WATLINGTON   TO PRINCES RISBOROUGH

70 FT

CHINNOR
3ᴹ 48ᶜ

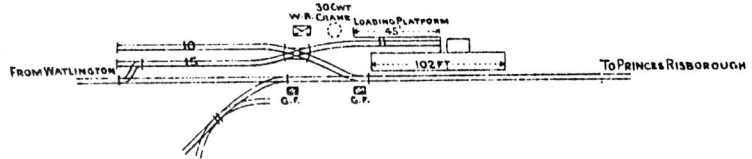

30 CWT
W.B. CRANE   LOADING PLATFORM
45'
10
FROM WATLINGTON   15   102 FT   TO PRINCES RISBOROUGH
G.F.   G.F.

KINGSTON CROSSING HALT
5ᴹ 8ᶜ

FROM WATLINGTON   TO PRINCES RISBOROUGH

70 FT

ASTON ROWANT
6ᴹ 7ᶜ

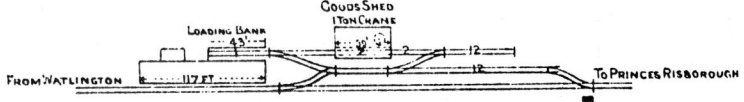

GOODS SHED
1 TON CRANE
LOADING BANK
43'
2   12
FROM WATLINGTON   117 FT   12   TO PRINCES RISBOROUGH

LEWKNOR BRIDGE HALT
6ᴹ 75ᶜ

FROM WATLINGTON   TO PRINCES RISBOROUGH

70 FT

WATLINGTON
8ᴹ 66ᶜ

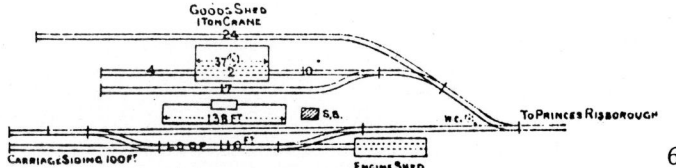

GOODS SHED
1 TON CRANE
24
37
4   2   10
17
138 FT   S.B.   W.C.   TO PRINCES RISBOROUGH
CARRIAGE SIDING 100 FT   LOOP 110'   ENGINE SHED

65

Schematic Station diagrams. *(Public Record Office)*

A Postwar aerial view of Princes Risborough. The Watlington and Thame lines curve away to the left, the Aylesbury branch diverges to the right, while the main line heads North toward Aynho Junction. *(Aerofilms)*

CHAPTER V

Train Services and Traffic

The Watlington and Princes Risborough's service of three mixed trains each way on weekdays was perpetuated for some years by the Great Western. In 1884, trains left Watlington at 9.00 a.m., 2.10 p.m. and 5.40 p.m., the return workings being at 10.30 a.m., 3.40 p.m. and finally 6.30 p.m. from Princes Risborough. The time booked for the journey was forty minutes, although it is hard to see how this schedule was adhered to if there were any number of wagons to be picked up at the intermediate stations. Notwithstanding, journey times were cut to 35 minutes the next year, with the first train up and the last down a further five minutes quicker. Efforts were probably made to keep goods carried by these two trains to a minimum. Official maximum loadings of goods wagons in addition to the passenger vehicles were eight on down trains and ten on up workings. The greater number permitted on Watlington to Risborough trains was, of course, in recognition of the slightly easier gradients ruling in that direction.

By 1890, journey time for what might today be deemed the two commuter trains was down to 25 minutes. This was a far from discreditable performance, since at Nationalisation the booked time was one minute greater. The comparison is not entirely fair, of course, as four halts had appeared in addition in the timetable by 1948. Against this, the 1890 trains were potentially mixed, with all that that implied in terms of loose couplings and dubious braking.

Improvements to the service were made in 1893. The morning up, evening down, and the afternoon return trip became passenger only, and the afternoon trains were also retimed to the 25 minutes taken by the first and last trains of the day. Two mixed trains remained, leaving Princes Risborough at 10.35 a.m. and Watlington at 5.50 p.m., and booked at 35 minutes as before. In addition, a goods working was introduced, leaving Watlington at 11.30 a.m. and returning from Risborough an hour later.

For the summer timetable of 1893 an early morning passenger working was added, although this was shortlived, and a total of four trains each way remained the norm until the turn of the Century. Details of the motive power the Great Western used to work the line in the '80s and '90s have not come to light, but four-coupled tank engines of Armstrong's "517" class were probably involved. With more certainty, passenger trains were composed of three four-wheeled carriages. Passenger trains were far from heavily

No. 7442 approaching Bledlow Bridge on a down train comprising horseboxes and autotrailer, in June 1951. *(R.F.G. Simpson)*

No. 4650 leaving Lewknor Bridge for Watlington, also post-nationalisation.
(Courtesy L. Nicholson)

loaded and goods traffic, particularly from the intermediate stations, increased in relative importance over the years. For the latter part of the decade before 1900, however, the one goods working in each direction was adequate for traffic from Chinnor and Aston Rowant, and mixed trains were precluded from picking up or dropping wagons at these stops to prevent undue extension of the journey time for passengers. The number of wagons was further restricted to six plus a brake van and the passenger vehicles.

In 1900, an additional train was incorporated in the timetable, and the goods working was cut back to run from Princes Risborough to Chinnor and back. With the addition of a Mondays only early passenger turn, Watlington departures became:

Passenger (MO)	Passenger	Mixed	Passenger	Mixed
7.40 a.m.	9.05 a.m.	10.55 a.m.	3.10 p.m.	6.35 p.m.

Trains were due to leave Risborough as follows:

Passenger (MO)	Mixed	Goods	Passenger	Passenger	Passenger
8.20 a.m.	9.52 a.m.	12.15 p.m.	1.10 p.m.	3.50 p.m.	7.30 p.m.

Journey times for passenger and mixed trains were unchanged, and the goods train was due to arrive at Chinnor at 12.25 p.m., returning fifteen minutes later. Goods traffic from Aston Rowant then had to be picked up by the down mixed train, most of it subsequently being returned to the junction by the up mixed trains, which were not permitted to pick up or uncouple goods wagons at Aston Rowant. This arrangement must clearly have proved inadequate, for soon after a further goods train was added after the arrival at Watlington of the 3.50 p.m. train, and this ran only as far as Aston Rowant before returning. Doubtless it was arranged in this fashion to prevent an undue gap between the two afternoon passenger workings, but it must still have resulted in some unnecessary wagon mileage and marshalling.

A statement emanating from the Engineer's Office at Paddington in 1902 described the type of engine used on the line as being a 0-4-2 passenger tank of the "517" class, but six-coupled saddle and subsequently pannier tanks in fact predominated from this time. Loads for the "517" class were officially limited to seven coal or mineral wagons, or ten goods wagons, or fourteen empties for up trains, and six, nine, or twelve wagons respectively on down workings. No. 1465 of the class worked on the branch so far as can be ascertained throughout 1902, in all but September of 1903, and until the beginning of April the next year. Thereafter, no further engines of this wheel arrangement were recorded as allocated to the line until the "517" class's more modern replacement, the 14xx series, appeared on the branch from time to time in post-Nationalisation days. It must, however, be added that engine allocations were only noted for records at one or perhaps two days in each month, and engines might therefore have appeared for odd days, or even for two or three weeks, without being recorded in this way.

Goods traffic became sufficiently intensive, or passenger complaints sufficiently vocal, for the antiquated practice of running mixed trains to be abandoned in October 1904. Four passenger trains were then run each way daily, leaving Watlington at 9.05, 11.45, 3.15 p.m. and 6.50, and Princes Risborough at 9.50, 1.10 p.m., 3.50 and 7.30. This left room for two goods workings in each direction, the first leaving Watlington at the early hour of 6.30 a.m. and returning in good time before the first passenger train, and the second at 4.30 p.m., returning from Risborough an hour later. At this date, twenty minutes only was the time for passenger trains between terminus and junction.

Despite the continued operation of the line on the one engine in steam principle indicated in the timetables, there appear to have been two engines allocated to Watlington — one passenger and one goods — at any one time from the turn of the Century down to September 1906. Quite how these were operated is not clear, although it is reasonable to suppose that the goods engine may have spent much of its time shunting in the yard at Princes Risborough which, of course, could be done without possession of the Watlington Branch train staff.

The goods engine was almost invariably one of the then newly-built "2021" class of 4ft.-wheeled six-coupled tank locos., and these later also worked the passenger trains until early British Railways days. The table lists all those recorded as allocated to Watlington, although the same comments that were made in relation to the "517" class apply equally here: others may have worked the line from time to time, but were not in evidence on the census dates. In contradistinction, the census day must on occasions have coincided with the changeover of motive power when the engines were returned, generally to Slough for boiler wash-out, and replaced by others. On one occasion, no less than four members of the "2021" class were officially noted as allocated to Watlington!

The first pannier tank conversion of the "2021" class recorded on the branch was No. 2159, converted in September 1916 and noted in October and November of that year, as well as at subsequent dates. With this exception, the dividing line between the class with saddle tanks and the modified engines with pannier tanks may be drawn in the summer of 1922. Before August when No. 2103 was allocated to Watlington, no pannier tank engines other than No. 2159 were in evidence: after that date, no saddle tanks were recorded.

After the "517" class, the 2-4-0 side tank locomotives of the "Metro" class became the passenger engine used, and these persisted off and on until 1926. Numbers and dates are shown in a further table.

Other classes of engines were seen on the branch on occasions. No. 639, one of twelve in the Wolverhampton-built "633" class of side tank engines replaced No. 1465 in September 1903. No. 1172, an outside-framed six-coupled saddle tank locomotive of the "Buffalo" class with 4ft. 6ins. wheels, was in evidence during parts of the years 1912-16. Except during the first of those years, so also was No. 1770 of Dean's "1701" class, also with 4ft. 6ins. wheels, and then running as a saddle tank with the original type of boiler with dome on the front section.

A further type of six-coupled tank locomotive seen on the line was the "1901" series, a shorter wheelbase antecedent of the "2021" class having in common the 4ft. wheel diameter. No. 1953, built in 1888, was recorded briefly during 1923 by which date it had been fitted with pannier tanks. The smaller wheeled varieties must generally have been regarded as the most suitable motive power, for the "2021" class were well-nigh ubiquitous, as has been seen, until more modern pannier tanks began to take over during the second war. These included the 57xx series, Nos. 5716 and 5783 being recorded during 1944, the 37xx and 46xx series and, in later years, engines of the 74xx class.

Steam railmotors are believed to have been tried out on the line when three halts were opened in September 1906. None were recorded as allocated to Watlington as such, but in all probability Oxford or Old Oak Common-based units came to be used: they were no doubt regarded as insufficiently robust to stand out in the open at Watlington, and too new in concept to be kept far from the eyes of experienced shed staff. The halts had low platforms only, so carriages of the conventional type could no longer be used on their own. Branch passenger trains from then on always included a railmotor or later an autotrailer, and these vehicles were provided

Watlington Motive Power - 1

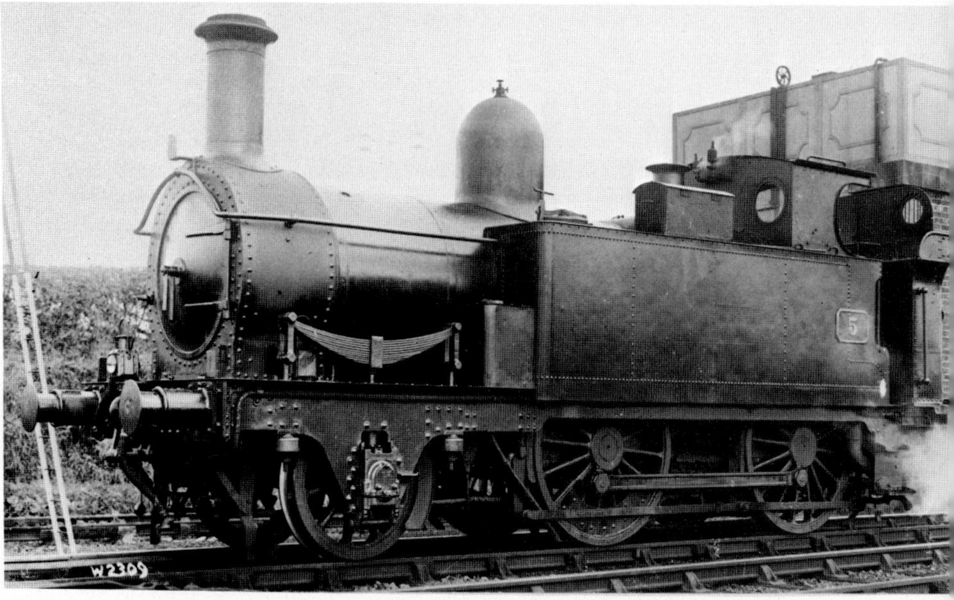

Passenger trains for a number of years were in the hands of "Metro" class 2-4-0Ts. No. 5 worked briefly on the branch in 1904.
(Real Photographs)

No. 1406 of the same class was allocated to Watlington in mid-1926
(Real Photographs)

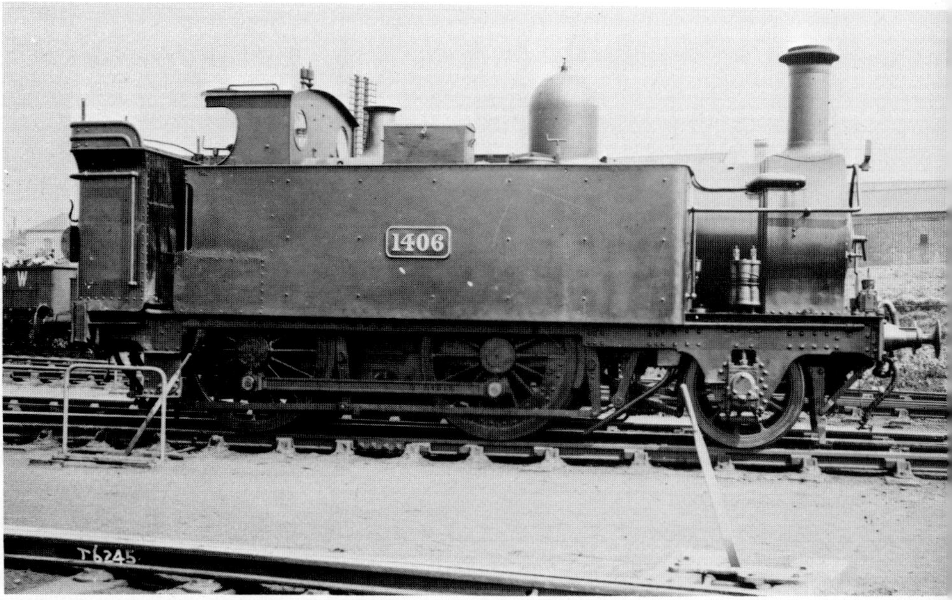

Mainstay on the branch for more than fifty years was the "2021" class 0-6-0T. No. 2072 worked the timetable in much the form illustrated during 1927 and 1928. *(Real Photographs)*

No. 2112 perhaps came closest to being the "Branch Engine" in the years after 1930, but it is here shown exemplifying the class in earlier days. No. 2112 itself acquired domed boiler and pannier tank in 1916. *(Loco and General Railway Photos.)*

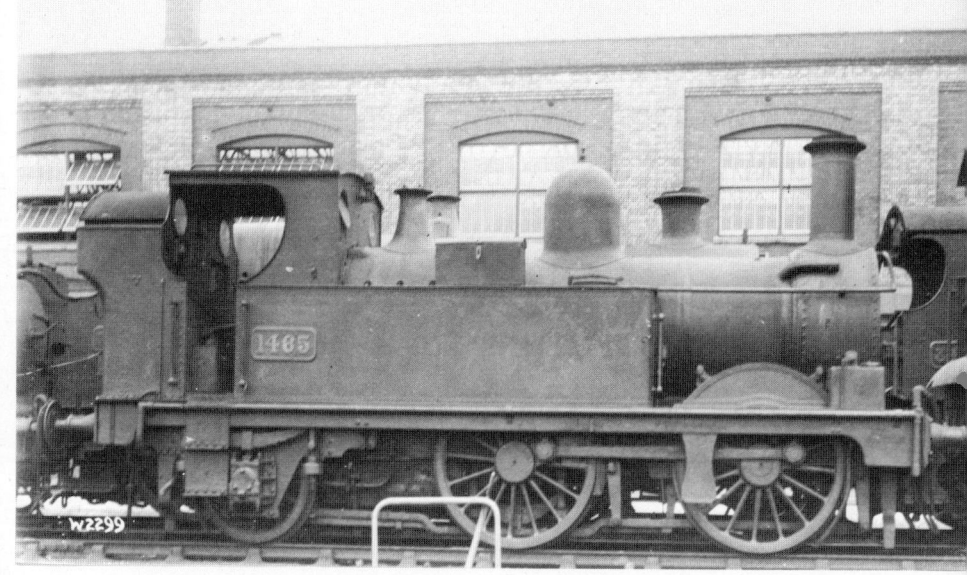

The "517" class 0-4-2T was specified for the line around the turn of the Century. No. 1465 was in evidence on passenger services in 1901-4, although it is here seen in much later condition. *(Real Photographs)*

— And Watlington Rolling Stock

A 1919 photograph of Watlington chiefly of interest for the coaching stock depicted: An early trailer conversion from a railmotor and a four-wheel brake 3rd, both in all-red livery, together with what appear to be two old "Siphon" vans. *(Loco and General Railway Photos)*

with retracting steps to allow them to set down passengers at halts.

Photographs point to trailer No. 117 being used on the line for at least part of the inter-war period. This was a 59ft. 6ins. vehicle with straight, match-boarded, sides converted from railmotor No. 21 in 1920 and fitted with Dean four point suspension bogies. The more modern flush-sided trailers of Collett's regime predominated in later years. A coach working programme of 1937 quotes a 70ft. branch car for Watlington, but trailers of this length were by no means exclusively used.

The additional stops necessitated a five minute increase in the journey time, but the service was improved in other respects by the introduction of additional trains. So, in October 1906, departures became:

From Watlington —

Goods (MO)	Goods (MX)	Pass. (MO)	Pass.	Pass.	Pass.	Pass.	Pass.	Goods
6.00 am	6.40	7.38	8.55	11.40	3.10 pm	4.30	6.55	8.05

And from Princes Risborough —

Goods (MO)	Goods (MX)	Pass. (MO)	Pass.	Pass.	Pass.	Pass.	Pass.	Goods
6.40 am	7.40	8.18	9.42	12.58 pm	3.48	5.19	7.30	9.40

Intermediate times were five minutes between Risborough and Bledlow Bridge, Bledlow Bridge and Chinnor, and four minutes from there to Kingston Crossing. Kingston Crossing to Aston Rowant and Aston Rowant to Lewknor Bridge each took three minutes, and finally from Lewknor to Watlington, five minutes. This pattern of train services remained very much the same for the next fifty years although various changes were made from time to time. The Mondays Only early morning working disappeared and reappeared in the timetable, for example, and during various periods up to the Second World War, the late goods from Princes Risborough was replaced on Saturdays by a passenger train. This connected with the 9.00 p.m. from Paddington and left Risborough at 10.25 initially, but in later years half an hour later.

The increasing traffic to Benton's lime works at Chinnor allowed a further freight working to be justified by 1920, and this left Princes Risborough just after noon and ran initially to Aston Rowant and back, but later only as far as Chinnor. Goods engines working on goods trains were allowed greater loads than those previously cited for passenger engines on the same duty. In either direction, ten loaded coal wagons or fifteen goods wagons or twenty empties were permitted. These were later increased 30% for down trains and 40% for up, with a tonnage limit of 168 tons for passenger engines and 224 tons for six-coupled locomotives. Officially, the branch could handle 40-wagon trains, but this would have necessitated locomotives more powerful than the "Group A" category quoted for the line. Goods trains carried a single lamp above the middle of the buffer beam, while passenger trains carried the "B" headcode.

In September 1925 a further halt was added between Bledlow Bridge and Chinnor, and this called for an extra minute in the timing. A thirty mile-per-hour speed limit on the branch discouraged the notion that this could be made up along the line! By that time, a Sunday milk train had been introduced: previously no trains ran on Sundays. Milk freighted from Watlington, centred as it was in the middle of an extensive agricultural area, grew to quite substantial proportions with receipts reaching £1,000 annually before much of it was lost to road competition.

The milk train left at 7.30 a.m. and returned from Princes Risborough at nine o'clock as a goods working, arriving at 10.10. Three minutes was allowed on the up journey at both Aston Rowant and Chinnor for the loading of more churns of milk.

On most Sundays the branch would then have relapsed into its traditional inactivity, but in 1926 the first of a number of Sunday excursions was organised. A great number of people were circulated by postcard with the suggestion "Come to Watlington and see the bluebells". 400 duly paid 4s.6d. a head for the excursion on April 25th from Paddington to Watlington and back. Coaches were worked through onto the branch, and the auto-trailer tacked on behind for those wishing to begin their botanical studies at one of the halts.

Further excursions were arranged subsequently at the appropriate time of year and thus was the "Bluebell Express" born, its not very original nickname at least making a change from the title of "Watlington Donkey" by which the branch train was known locally. The "Bluebell Express" continued to be well supported, and a press report cited 300 passengers on the Sunday train run on May 11th

Stationmaster Pocock about to give the "right away" to unidentified "2021" class 0-6-0T and autotrailer No. 117, about 1930. *(Courtesy Mrs. Clarke & Mrs. Watts)*

1930. In due course, excursions were also run from Watlington to various seaside resorts, thereby bringing welcome additional traffic to the line.

There was some curtailment of passenger services by 1940, but by the end of the war the number of passenger trains was restored to five each way, with an additional working at just after noon on Saturdays displacing the goods train to Chinnor until later in the afternoon. Departures were then:

From Watlington —

Goods	Pass.	Pass.	Pass.	Pass.(SO)	Pass.	Pass.	Goods
4.20 am	7.25	8.42	11.30	1.15 pm	3.10	7.15	8.50

And from Princes Risborough —

Goods	Empty Auto	Pass.	Goods(SX)	Pass.(SO)
5.30 am	7.57	10.22	12.20 pm	12.40

Pass.	Goods(SO)	Pass.	Pass.	Goods
1.55	3.55	5.55	8.02	10.45

The midday goods was due to leave Chinnor at 1.18 p.m., or 4.55 on Saturdays, and the evening goods ran as required. Although billed as an empty stock movement, the return leg of the first passenger train of the day was in fact permitted to carry passengers if there were any who wished to avail themselves of the facility. The final timetable of the Great Western period included another goods trip to run, when required, as far as Chinnor and back. This was timed between the arrival of the 8.42 a.m. from Watlington and the departure of the 10.22.

For many years there were one or two good connections for the Watlington branch to and from London trains at Princes Risborough. It was, for example, possible to catch the train which left Watlington at around 8.40 a.m. and be at Paddington at ten. It was equally possible shortly before the second war to catch the 6.50 p.m. and not reach London until 2 hours and 40 minutes later, having meandered via Maidenhead in the meantime! In the other direction, a coach was slipped at Risborough from the 7.10 p.m. Birmingham train, and it was thus possible to arrive in this rather distinctive fashion until towards the end of the era of slipcoach operation. At Princes Risborough, slip coaches were brought to a stop outside the station, and hauled into the platform by the yard engine. The best time by conventional means, again in the prewar period, was one and a half hours by the 4.40 p.m., which allowed Watlington to be reached at 6.11 p.m.

The inevitable pannier tank and autotrailer approach Aston Rowant under an overcast sky in 1940. *(Mr. & Mrs. Scott)*

No. 7441 runs round its trailer at Watlington in the last years of operation, and then propels the coach back into the platform. *(Lens of Sutton)*

Passenger traffic showed a predictable decline over the years, although not in this case for the usual reason of a competing bus service. There was no bus service between Watlington, Chinnor and Risborough while the line remained open for passenger traffic and Chinnor in particular was always badly served by bus routes of any sort.

A typical week in 1913 produced an average of twenty passengers per train for all up trains, and an identical figure for Watlington-bound services. The Mondays-only early morning train was well below average, and on the Monday in question carried only four passengers returning from Princes Risborough. The maximum number recorded on any individual train was sixty-eight. Ten years later, a sample week produced a similar average for down workings, but less than nine passengers on average for each of the trains from Watlington, a figure which was probably atypically low for some reason.

In general, the first train up and the last down were the best patronised, and the mid-afternoon service from Princes Risborough was also well used. By the 1930's, passengers carried dropped to an average of ten or eleven, and on a depressingly large percentage of the week's trains, the number could be counted on the fingers of one hand. The first train of the day from Watlington was by then accounting for more than 40% of those travelling in that direction, but even so did not exceed forty passengers. This train acquired a regular clientele, and the story is widely told that it was customary practice for passengers and staff to check amongst themselves that all the regulars were present, a porter frequently being dispatched to the station gates to look if any latecomers could be sighted hurrying up the road. This courtesy was returned to the extent of telephoning the station to advise that some regular passenger would not be travelling so that the train should not be delayed on his account.

Until the decline of passenger traffic in the 1930's, an additional coach was kept at Watlington and regularly used to supplement the accommodation provided by the autotrailer. The vehicle allocated in 1924 forms the background in the station group photograph, from which it would appear to be a three compartment brake third with four wheels, and of the conventional branch line type. Passengers travelling to or from the halts could not, of course, use this vehicle. The previously mentioned coach working programme of 1937 specified a six-wheel brake third carriage, while local residents recall a rather longer vehicle of perhaps seven or eight compartments as the spare coach.

The working of an extra carriage or other tail traffic in addition to the autotrailer did not in any way upset operation, since it was normal practice to run round the train at both ends of the journey. As there was frequently shunting work to be done between passenger trains, very little extra in the way of coupling and uncoupling was called for, and there was equally no need to allocate an auto-fitted engine to the Branch.

With the introduction of railcars, branch trains became one class only. It appears, however, that first class accommodation may have been laid on to order, or at least some system of reserved compartments instituted. Mr. Pocock, stationmaster at Watlington for more than twenty years, recalled that when he first held that position in 1924, there were still paper first class tickets of Watlington and Princes Risborough Railway origin in use. The validity of these was apparently questioned by ticket collectors on the main line, and so Mr. Pocock had them withdrawn soon after.

A recollection from a different source and dating from around 1910 is of Lady Plowden arriving at Aston Rowant station from Aston House in a dog-cart, complete with retinue, and being bowed into "her own" carriage. This carriage was apparently worked through to London, a manoeuvre not commonly undertaken for passenger vehicles.

Milk traffic has already been mentioned. Some twelve to fifteen farmers brought milk to Watlington, and this was loaded from the end of the platform, generally into six-wheel "Siphon" vans, which were worked through with the first train of the day. One van was loaded for Paddington and a second for Kensington. Other goods traffic from Watlington was also mostly of agricultural origin. The greatest volume was in hay and straw, (sometimes amounting to six or seven wagon-loads a day), sugar beet and livestock. There were also substantial quantities of watercress moved to Birmingham, Wolverhampton and Manchester, also frequently in Siphon vans, and more unusual traffic in the form of live pheasants and pheasants' eggs. These came mostly from England's Game Farm at Christmas Common, and were dispatched to all parts of the country, including the York Moors for hatching. In the other direction, the traffic was mostly coal, anthracite, animal feeding stuffs, and livestock, including sheep from Scotland and lambs from Kent. There were also two vans daily, one from Paddington and one from Oxford, with small consignments for traders at Watlington.

Coal was brought mostly from west midland collieries, either in colliery owned wagons — Griff, Spiers, Baddesley, Bright (Derby) and Moira (Staffordshire) have been mentioned — or in coal factors' wagons. Anthracite and Furnacite, along with locomotive coal, came from Wales. None of the local coal merchants operated their own wagons. Weedon Bros. worked from the coal yard at the station for many years until the firm went out of business during the second world war, and Fred. Hoare was the other coal merchant operating during the early years of the century. He ceased trading around 1920, about which time Stanmore Brothers and Tappin and Sons started in business. The latter took over the coal yard from Weedon and ultimately became the only merchant remaining in the town. Tappins' trade amounted to between fifty and sixty tons a week, and as well as supplying customers within about six miles radius of Watlington, the firm carted to Shirburn Castle, Watlington Park, and some of the other major estates which bought coal direct.

During the second world war, an Ordnance Depot was built near the station, and this, together with the USAAF base at Chalgrove, gave rise to a fair amount of activity, necessitating special workings from time to time. On occasions, consignments for Chalgrove required the use of the base's own mobile crane, the individual loads being beyond the capability of the Watlington yard crane.

At Aston Rowant, as well as freight in agricultural products, livestock and coal, there was at one time a quite substantial traffic in wooden furniture and turned chair components. This emanated from factories at Stokenchurch and workshops on the wooded ridge of the Chilterns between Stokenchurch and Aston Rowant. Aston Rowant was also notable for the working of horseboxes, either as tail traffic or by special train when justified, for horses passing through the Aston Park stud.

Chinnor was the busiest station on the branch for freight, with regular daily consignments of coal and gypsum required at the lime and cement works, and loads of timber for the yard on the north side of the line. Around 100 tons of coal a month was railed to the works between 1908 and 1919, during which period only lime was produced. With the start of cement manufacturing the demand for coal tripled, and gypsum accounted for a further 100 tons a month, all this fuel and raw material coming from the Midlands. Requirements grew as the cement works expanded, so that by 1927 some 1,000 tons of coal a month and roughly a quarter that quantity of gypsum came to Chinnor, increasing by the end of the Great Western period to around 2,700 tons of fuel a month and a proportionate amount of gypsum. In earlier years most of the lime and cement produced found its way out by rail, but the growth of

An aerial view of Chinnor Cement Works taken in August 1937. *(Aerofilms)*

No. 7442 nearing Watlington with the train seen earlier at Bledlow Bridge.
(R.F.G. Simpson)

Sheepcote Lane, Lewknor, now truncated by Motorway developments. The halt was approached by steps beside the left-hand bridge abutment, and hidden by the trees in this photograph *(Courtesy C.M. Strevens)*

road transit gradually eroded this position, so that by 1940 no more than 50% was despatched by train. Ten years later, rail offtake had virtually ceased.

The offloading of timber at Chinnor was much less regular, depending as it did on the arrival of imports. A substantial proportion was beech from France and this came with the tree-trunks already rough sawn into planks. Unlike the cement works, the timber yard did not have its own rail access, and loads had to be doublehandled from the loading bay at the station onto trailers and thence into the works. Since the closure of the line for freight other than to Chinnor Cement at the beginning of 1961, timber has been brought in by road.

The use of towropes in the sidings at Chinnor was permitted in the early years of the century, and the 1922 Sectional Appendix warned against engines passing over the wagon weighbridge there.

The working of the branch on the one engine in steam principle made for little in the way of operating complexity, except on the infrequent occasions when the services of a breakdown train or snowplough were required. Then, before the service train from Slough could enter the line, the train staff had to be taken to Princes Risborough by other means. This was not always without its problems. One instance is recorded of the branch train being snowed up — the track around Kingston and beyond being particularly liable to drifts — when all the roads of the area were equally snowbound. A porter, despatched with the staff, had to make his way on foot as best he could, and his non-appearance at Risborough until many hours later caused great concern.

The train staff for the branch incorporated an Annett's Key, and this was required to unlock ground frames at Chinnor and Aston Rowant, as well as the door of the hut containing the frame for Benton's sidings at Chinnor. At Watlington, point and locking levers were contained in a building which was hardly a ground frame but whose diminutive size scarcely suggested the title of signal box. In later years, this apparently contained only four levers. Photographs indicate that these were arranged with one operating the point leading to the goods yard, together with a trap point in the yard, a second lever providing the necessary locking for a facing point on a running line. Another worked the junction end of the loop in conjunction with entry to the locomotive road, effectively as if the points constituted a crossover. An economy lever was used here, a comparative rarity, combining the operation of the two points with

Aston Rowant Station soon after nationalisation. Charlie Hopkins in attendance.
(Courtesy C. Hopkins)

87

Ex-Great Eastern Railway 0-6-0 No. 65390 on a Chinnor working at Princes Risborough in April 1958. *(Courtesy R.C. Riley)*

the provision of a facing point lock for the first-mentioned. The Watlington end of the loop was linked with the carriage siding in similar fashion, except that no locking was required, and these two points were controlled by the final lever in the frame. In the goods yard, the remaining points were worked by adjacent hand levers.

A number of signals were installed by the Great Western on the branch. Having cleared the Risborough starter and the bracket signal protecting a crossover to the Thame line, the first branch signal was located at Kingston, nearly 400 yards short of the level crossing it protected and on the right hand side of the track for Watlington trains. The next was the Watlington fixed distant at Shirburn, on the same side of the line and approximately 500 yards before the station platform according to the large-scale Ordnance Survey. Finally, there was the Watlington home signal by the facing points for the goods yard, and on the other side of the line. Up trains first cleared the starter by Watlington signal box, but met no more signals before the Kingston distant, about 500 yards short of the crossing and on the up side. The Risborough distant was roughly half way round the curve bringing the branch parallel with the Thame line, with the home some ten chains before Risborough North Box.

The two distant signals at Kingston crossing were required because the gates were normally kept open for road traffic across the railway, and these signals were retained after the others on the branch were removed. They were unusual for Great Western practice in having lattice posts, and according to the 1922 Sectional Appendix were not interlocked with the gates, although this provision is reported to have been made at a later date.

Signals were not required at Wainhill as the road here was of a very minor character, and the crossing was left clear for the railway. Currently, however, the gates at Wainhill are kept across the track since traffic to the cement works calls for their opening rarely more than twice daily. Prominent signs require trains to stop at the crossing for the gates to be opened.

To the casual observer the branch may well have exhibited the somnolence typically imputed to rural lines of its kind, but for the engine crews, the requirements of timetable and traffic meant that their day was far from easy. Mr. Humphries, a driver on the Watlington branch from 1924 until only shortly before passenger services were withdrawn, recalled that there were few idle moments during the day. Shunting was frequently required in the intervals between the arrival of one passenger train at Watlington and its subsequent departure, and equally, the branch engine was also required to work the yard at Princes Risborough. A more unusual activity was the use of the engine to pump water from the well, which is still in evidence at Watlington, up to the water tower, and this continued until the electric pump was installed.

During those years when an early morning goods trip was worked, the first driver booked on at 4.50 a.m., this allowing him an hour to prepare the engine and train. The relief driver came on for the 3 p.m. departure from Watlington and finished the day with the late goods. According to the load, this train might return to the terminus at any time between that booked and around midnight. The tendency was always to deal with as much as possible on this working rather than on the early morning goods, as the morning trip had to be worked strictly to time. This was to allow the first passenger train of the day to depart on schedule, and merited a special note to that effect in the working timetables.

Three firemen were required, the third working through the night to keep the fire in and have steam up for the first train of the following day. Loco crews prepared to work from Watlington became increasingly hard to come by, and the story was reported in the national press of services being suspended while a fireman was on honeymoon. Apparently though, a relief fireman could be found to waft the newly-married couple away by train, making the whole affair sound somewhat implausible. What is beyond dispute is that in the three or four years before closure at Watlington, the branch engine was no longer "shedded" at the terminus, but worked light each day from and back to Slough. The change was attributed to the calling-up of one regular fireman for national service, but at least part of the reason was almost certainly an attempt to rationalise and reduce operating overheads. Prior to this, engines were sent every weekend to Slough for boiler wash-out.

ALLOCATION OF LOCOMOTIVES TO WATLINGTON, 1902-44.

"2021" CLASS 0-6-0T.

No.	Years	No.	Years
2026	1928, 1931, 1937-9	2098	1934
2046	1931-2, 1935-6	2103	1909-12, 1922-8
2055	1939, 1940, 1942-3	2112	1930-1, 1934, 1936-7, 1939-44
2069	1929, 1931	2113	1910-16
2072	1927-8	2121	1916-27
2074	1929, 1930, 1935	2126	1906-9
2078	1939, 1940-4	2132	1906-9
2081	1902-4, 1906, 1934	2137	1916-22
2083	1904-7	2150	1906-9
2087	1928-9, 1931-2, 1938	2159	1909-26

"METRO" CLASS 2-4-0T.

No.	Years	No.	Years
4	1904-6	3500	1913-4
5	1904	3561	1926
463	1903	3562	1913
613	1910	3563	1914, 1922
615	1909	3565	1922
616	1926	3566	1916, 1922
1406	1926	3569	1914
1408	1914-5	3584	1915
1417	1913	3587	1921
1460	1912-3	3595	1913

Note: All years in which a particular locomotive was recorded are shown, irrespective of whether the allocation was for only one of the recording dates during the year, or for the major part of a year.

CHAPTER VI

Decline and Closure

The wartime upsurge in traffic was for the most part short-lived, as a glance at some selected traffic statistics for the branch will show. The requirements of the Chinnor cement works continued to grow, as did parcels traffic from Watlington where a mail order business was established. The revenue from parcels was, however, lost by 1954, in which year receipts from passenger and parcels traffic for the three stations and four halts came to only £2,500, Aston Rowant contributing less than 5% to this total and Chinnor over 50%.

	1935	1943	1950
Passenger receipts	£1,744	£5,263	£2,882
Parcels receipts	£1,098	£ 682	£1,740
Number of tickets issued	16,672	60,458	20,904
Freight, to and from Chinnor	31,015 tons	31,987 tons	45,536 tons
Freight, other stations	12,559 tons	19,173 tons	7,460 tons

Costs, on the other hand, continued to rise. As an example the wages bill for the branch will suffice. In 1935, this was £1,750 for a staff of 12, an average of £146 p.a. per head. In 1943, the figure was £3,160 with 16 employed, an average just short of £200 each, while in 1950 the total had become £4,080 for the same number, £255 per man.

This was clearly a situation which could not be allowed to continue so far as the railway authorities were concerned, and it soon became common knowledge in the locality that the future of the branch was in the balance. A letter appeared in a national newspaper in 1951 bemoaning that the "Watlington Flyer" was to be replaced by a bus service, and pointing out that never would any bus operator emulate the very personal service provided by the railway.

Various economy measures were tried, but none could really combat the fundamental problem of insufficient passenger traffic to justify maintenance of the service, and insufficient goods movement except to Chinnor to warrant retention of facilities at Watlington and Aston Rowant. The number of staff was progressively reduced, and Watlington and Aston Rowant stations were "demoted" and became the responsibility of a chief porter. On the locomotive side, a six-coupled tank engine of Great Eastern Railway origin from

Aylesbury shed was tried early in 1955 with a view to reducing the light engine working previously required when a Slough engine was used. This experiment was not, however, successful.

Rumours of impending closure continued to circulate and, despite the opposition of the local councils, these were confirmed in October 1956. The last passenger train ran on Saturday June 29th 1957, the halts being closed from that date but the stations remaining open for parcels traffic. The train was hauled by pannier tank engine No. 4650 with driver William Thomas and fireman Brian Stickland, and consisted of the customary branch car with guard Don Gray, and an ex-GWR corridor third class coach. A large crowd including the Chairman and six members of the parish council gathered at Chinnor to witness the end of almost 85 years of passenger operations on the branch, and around seventy people joined the train there to make a final journey to Watlington and back.

At Watlington, more people had gathered including the acting stationmaster Mr. K. Lewis, Mr. Frank Hyde, who began working at the station in 1920 and was related by marriage to the first stationmaster there, and Mr. Tom Tunnicliffe. These three remained at Watlington after the closure to passenger traffic and were responsible for the freight trains that continued to use the line. The last passenger working returned towards Princes Risborough to the accompaniment of the customary detonators, being greeted at Chinnor by the equally obligatory refrains of "Auld Lang Syne". The trains were replaced by buses operated by City of Oxford Motor Services.

Freight traffic did not long outlast passenger operations, for the Western Region was given permission to withdraw the service from the section beyond Chinnor from January 2nd 1961. During the early part of the intervening period a "J-15" class 0-6-0 was employed on freight trains, the only recorded instance of a tender engine being used on the branch. Nos. 65390 and 65405 were allocated to Aylesbury to work on the line from late 1957, 65390 later being replaced by 65452. Track was lifted early in 1963, operations being centred on Aston Rowant where 20ft. lengths of track were piled for subsequent removal by road. Having commenced demolition from Chinnor, the contractor's crane, wagons and locomotive had also to be taken away by road.

The line from the junction to just beyond Chinnor station remained, and is still in operation today to provide the raw material and fuel required at the Cement works. Much of this section was

A more than usually crowded scene at Watlington, taken during the last week of operation. (*Lens of Sutton*)

Another typical view at the terminus, on account both of the unusual large number of enthusiasts among the passengers and of the rare appearance on the branch of a 14xx class 0-4-2T.

(Lens of Sutton)

relaid with concrete sleepers and flat-bottom rail in 1960, and the track is well-ballasted and far from overgrown. The low-level platforms at Bledlow Bridge and Wainhill halts are still in evidence, but all the other fittings at these two locations have been removed. The station building at Chinnor was demolished in recent years and the platform has also been broken up.

There are, however, a number of relics from the very early days of the railway still to be seen on the section between Chinnor and the junction, in the shape of rail fence supports. Two types are in use. The first is a flat-bottom rail of very light section, which appears to correspond closely to that used by the Watlington company and described in the 1883 report. The second was once broad-gauge "bridge" rail. It has been suggested that the Great Western actually relaid the W. & P.R. Railway with bridge section rails on longitudinal sleepers as a temporary measure prior to substitution of conventional trackwork, but it is equally probable that rail scrapped during gauge conversion elsewhere on the system was brought in solely for use in fencing.

The track layout at Chinnor station has been progressively simplified and now consists only of the loop and approximately 400 yards of rails extending towards Aston Rowant. There are two connections with the Cement Company's lines, the access to British Railways track at the Princes Risborough end being protected by a very short siding road terminating in a wooden stop-block.

Within the works boundary there is a further loop, roughly parallel with the loop surviving from the former station plan, and splitting into three sidings at the Watlington end. The first runs in front of all the buildings and is currently disused. The second terminates in a shed and could be utilised for the loading of bagged cement should this be required by rail at any future date, and the third runs behind the shed and over a wagon tippler before rejoining the first siding and making a further connection with British Railways track. The original sidings curving to the south towards the lime kilns are no longer in evidence.

The Cement Company's lines are on a falling gradient towards Watlington, as are the rails of the former Watlington branch up to the point where the second connection with the works sidings is made, when the gradient reverses. This allows operation to be very much simplified from what would otherwise be the case. Trains of up to twenty loaded mineral wagons are brought into the station loop and the engine runs round, recoupling at the other end and shunting the wagons into the works loop. There they are held on the handbrakes and allowed to run under gravity one at a time to the tippler. Once emptied, each wagon then runs once again under gravity to the end of the siding beyond the second connection to the branch, this spur having a capacity of just twenty wagons clear of the point blades which are spring loaded for access from the branch.

In the meantime, the train engine uncouples the brake van which runs freely along the branch to beyond the crossover leading into the lower end of the works. The engine then goes forward over the crossover to withdraw the previous day's wagons, now emptied, from the spur, the very minimum of locomotive working within cement company bounds thereby being required.

Midland Region Class 2 2-6-2 tank engines were employed on Chinnor goods rosterings before the present-day diesel motive power. Diesel operation was originally in the hands of North British type 2 locomotives of the 6300 number series, now scrapped and replaced by "Hymek" type 3's. These have also now been scrapped and the 12-wheeled Brush type 2 diesel-electric locomotives of the 5500 number series are employed on the line. In the mid-1960's, the branch working formed part of the duties of an Old Oak Common based locomotive which hauled an early-morning freight from Acton to Wycombe and Risborough, picking up loaded wagons at Risborough for a trip over the branch, and subsequently returning the empties. According to the dictates of the load available, a second trip to Chinnor might be required in the morning, the rest of the day's working being taken up with shunting at Wycombe and hauling oil tank wagons to the Shellmex and BP depot at Thame. The locomotive finished the day returning empty tank wagons to Acton.

This particular mode of operation no longer applies, however, and branch freight trains, although still arriving at Chinnor mid-morning, are not now an invariable occurrence each weekday. This does not imply any phasing out of rail haulage of incoming minerals and, on the contrary, plans are in hand to extend the siding facilities in the cement works to allow "presflos" or vans used for outgoing consignments to be held separately from empty mineral wagons.

At the time of writing, coal is brought via the Midland route to Acton, rather than by way of Banbury. Having worked an early trip to Greenford and back, the Old Oak Common-based locomotive picks up loaded mineral wagons at Acton, leaving there at 6.55 a.m. Arrival at Risborough is just under two hours later, with an intermediate stop to set down wagons at Wycombe North Yard.

Cement Works Traffic - 1

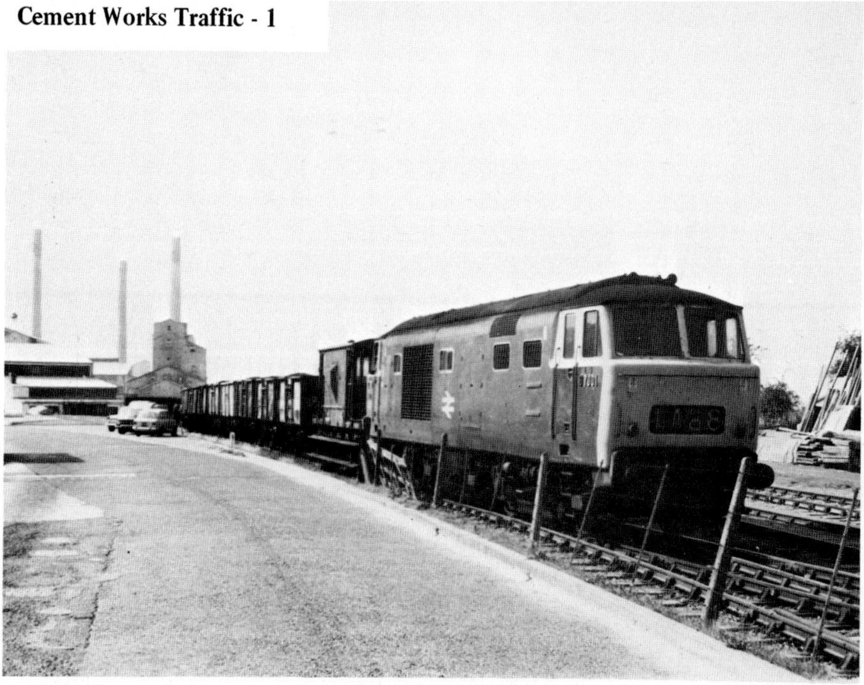

The line remained open as far as the Chinnor Cement Works after the closure to other traffic in 1961. A "Hymek" propels loaded coal wagons into the works (above) while on another day a North British Type 2 waits to set back to pick up empties. *(Courtesy G. Gamble)*

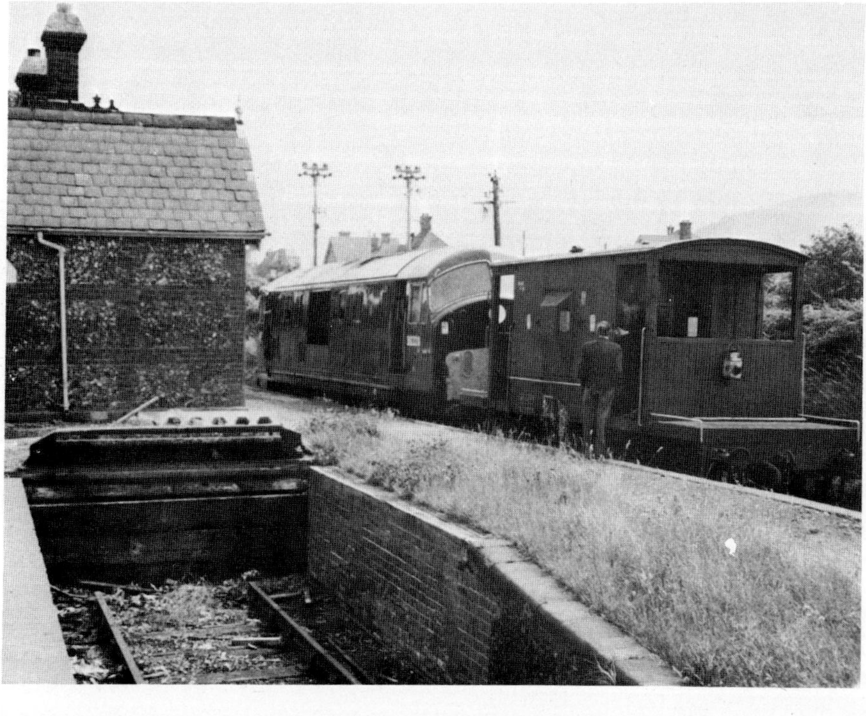

The second man prepares to alight at Wainhill to open the Crossing Gates for a North British Type 2 returning to the junction (above). Another of the same class is seen (below) heading for Chinnor to pick up empties, at the point where the branch diverts from the Thame line. *(Courtesy G. Gamble)*

Either one or two trips down the branch follow, booked to arrive at Chinnor at 9.29 and 11.34 a.m., before the return working with empties from Risborough and Wycombe to Acton. On Fridays, the turn is extended to include an evening freight to Exeter and Barnstaple, arriving back at noon the next day and leaving the locomotive spare on Sundays.

Much of the course of the line beyond Chinnor can still be readily traced. As far as Aston Rowant the trackbed is intact, although all sign of the halt at Kingston Crossing has disappeared apart from the crossing keeper's house. Aston Rowant station has been demolished and the site is now used by the County Council as a dump for road grit. The outline of the bay and lengths of platform railings remain in evidence nonetheless, as of necessity does the bridge under the Oxford Road.

Until mid-1972, the line could then be followed from the cutting beyond Aston Rowant station and the Oxford Road bridge, across the fields towards Lewknor Bridge Halt. The M40 motorway, however, now crosses the course of the Watlington branch on a high embankment, necessitating the diversion of the Watlington road. Together, these works have completely disrupted the previously existing contours of the area around the halt, and obliterated the brickwork of Lewknor bridge as well as the approach road from the village; these features remained after the halt itself and bridge girders had been removed at an earlier date.

The trackbed can only be traced again after an interval of roughly half a mile, from a point where it curves away from the new road to Watlington in the cutting which once commenced immediately beyond Lewknor Bridge Halt. For much of the intervening distance to the terminus the adjoining fields have been refenced to absorb the land formerly occupied by the railway. Towards Shirburn, however, the course of the line has been maintained as a private road, surfaced in part, to provide access within the adjacent estate.

At Watlington itself, all metal fittings were soon removed for scrap, but the major structures are still standing, albeit in somewhat dilapidated condition and unlikely to remain much longer before demolition. The station building, platform and goods shed have been used from time to time for the storage of farm materials, and the carriage shed could almost have been built for this purpose, being easily mistaken for a farm building from a distance. Indeed, the station has blended to such an extent into the surroundings and

No. 4650 on the last passenger train on the Watlington branch, 27 June 1957, passing a bay at Princes Risborough. *(Courtesy Mr. R.H. Siarey)*

is so remote from where a station serving the town might logically be expected to be that only the most observant passer-by would probably notice it.

This, then, is where the Watlington branch must be left after more than one hundred years of operation. The line can claim no records, no unique occurrences, no especial place in the transport and social history of Britain. Its significance derives from being so typical of the many railways which once provided an unspectacular service and filled an unassuming but important role in rural communities up and down the country, and which are no longer considered relevant to present-day transport needs.

Architectural Details.

Aston Rowant. Goods shed and station building both show minor differences from Watlington, notably in the chimneys. *(Courtesy J. Russell)*

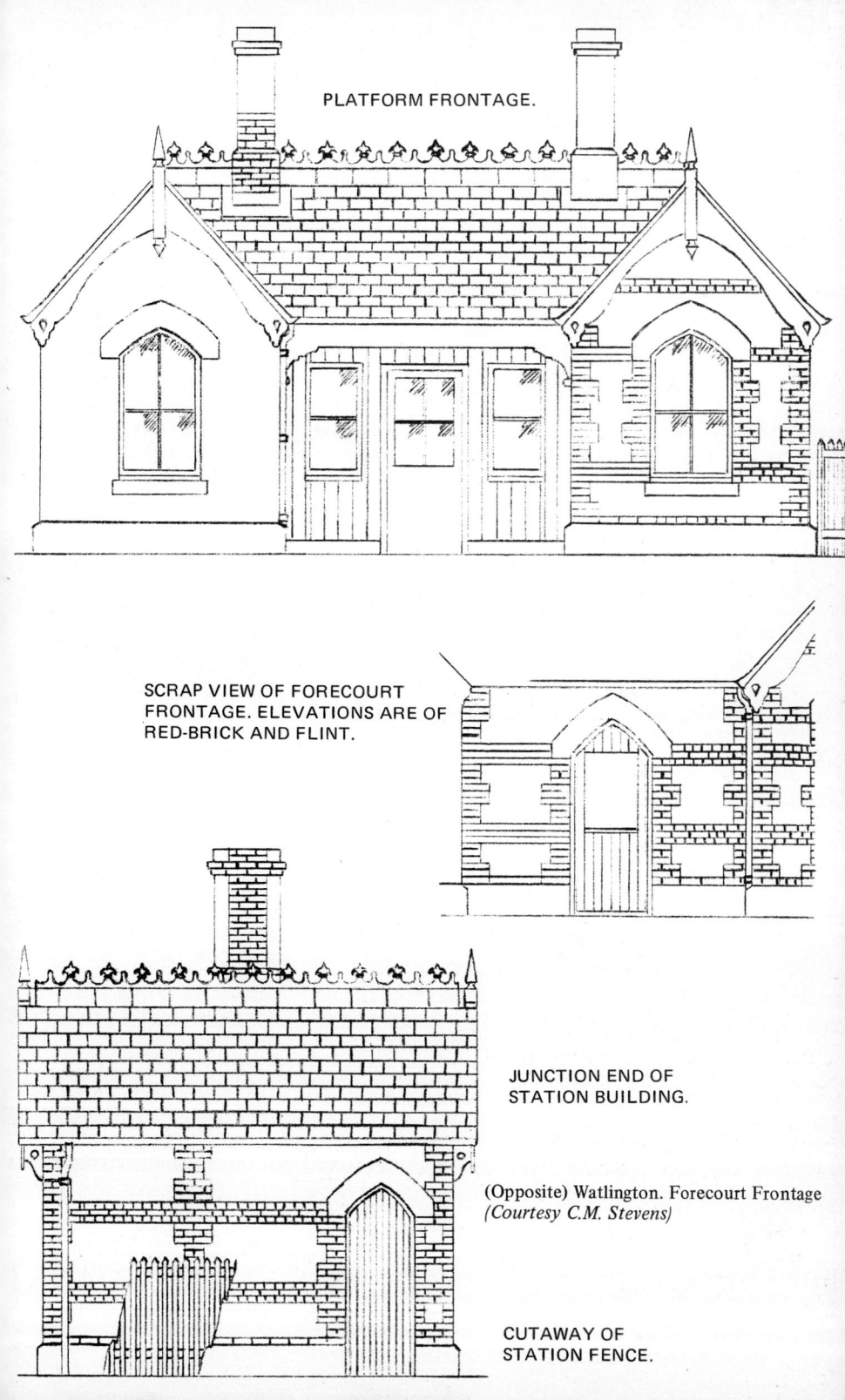

PLATFORM FRONTAGE.

SCRAP VIEW OF FORECOURT
FRONTAGE. ELEVATIONS ARE OF
RED-BRICK AND FLINT.

JUNCTION END OF
STATION BUILDING.

(Opposite) Watlington. Forecourt Frontage
(Courtesy C.M. Stevens)

CUTAWAY OF
STATION FENCE.

FLOORPLAN OF
STATION BUILDING.

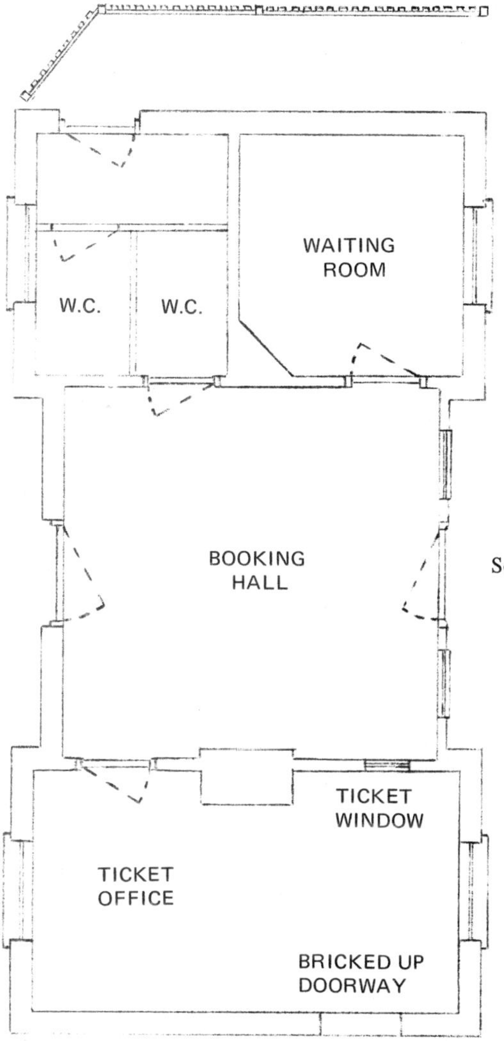

WAITING
ROOM

W.C. W.C.

BOOKING
HALL

Scale for all drawings
4mm to 1 ft.

TICKET
WINDOW

TICKET
OFFICE

BRICKED UP
DOORWAY

THE CARRIAGE SHED OF SIX EQUAL BAYS, DRAWN FROM
ON-SITE MEASUREMENTS AND PHOTOGRAPHS, SHOWS MINOR
DIFFERENCES FROM DIMENSIONS GIVEN IN THE 1883 REPORT.

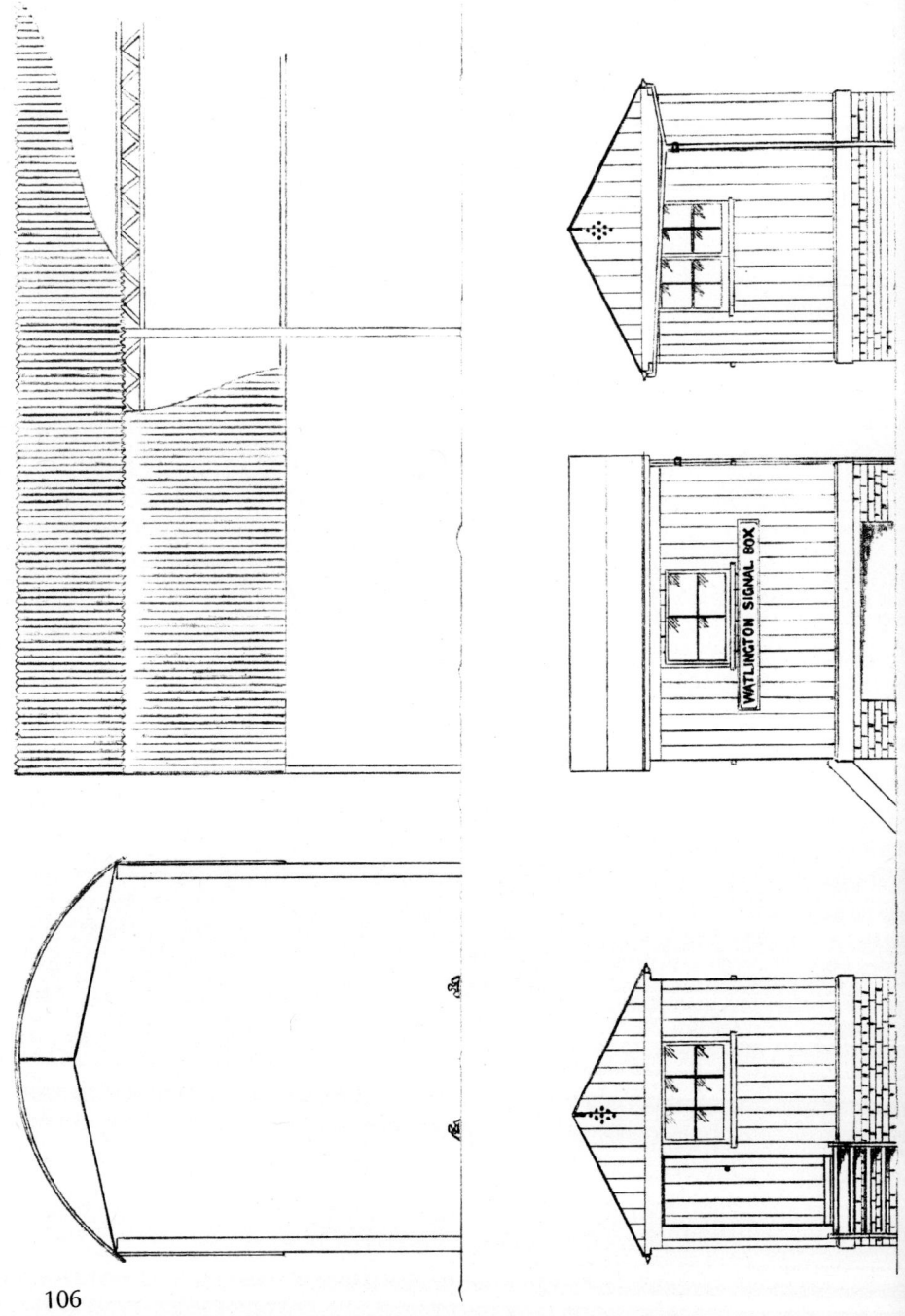

WATLINGTON SIGNAL BOX

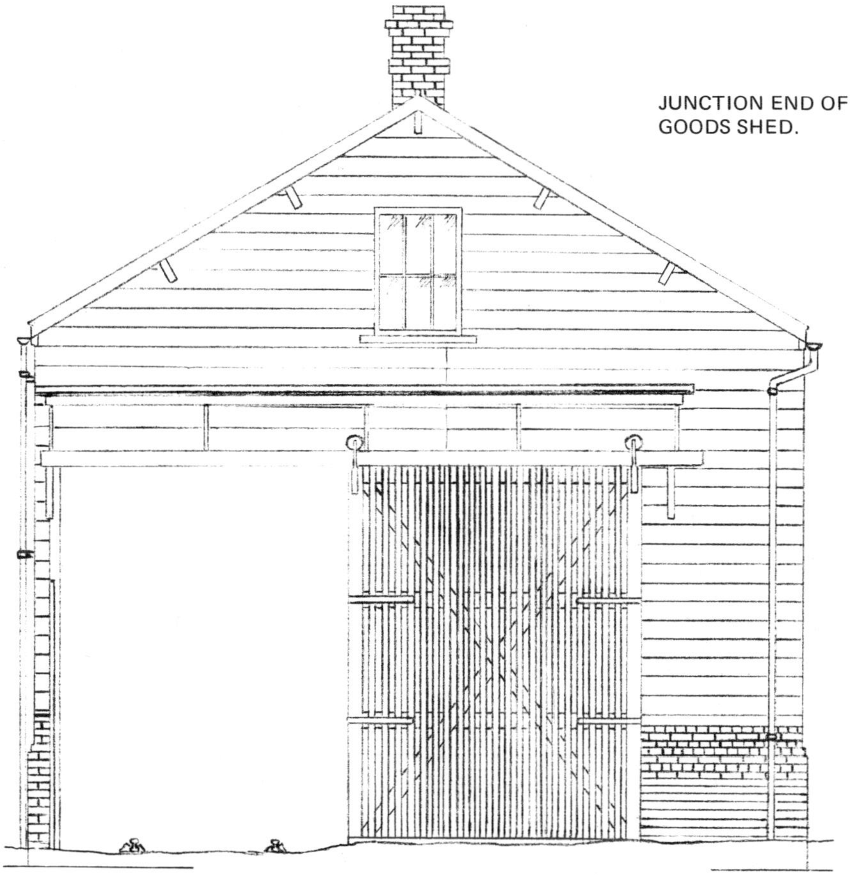

Part View of Goods Shed.

(Courtesy C.M. Strevens)

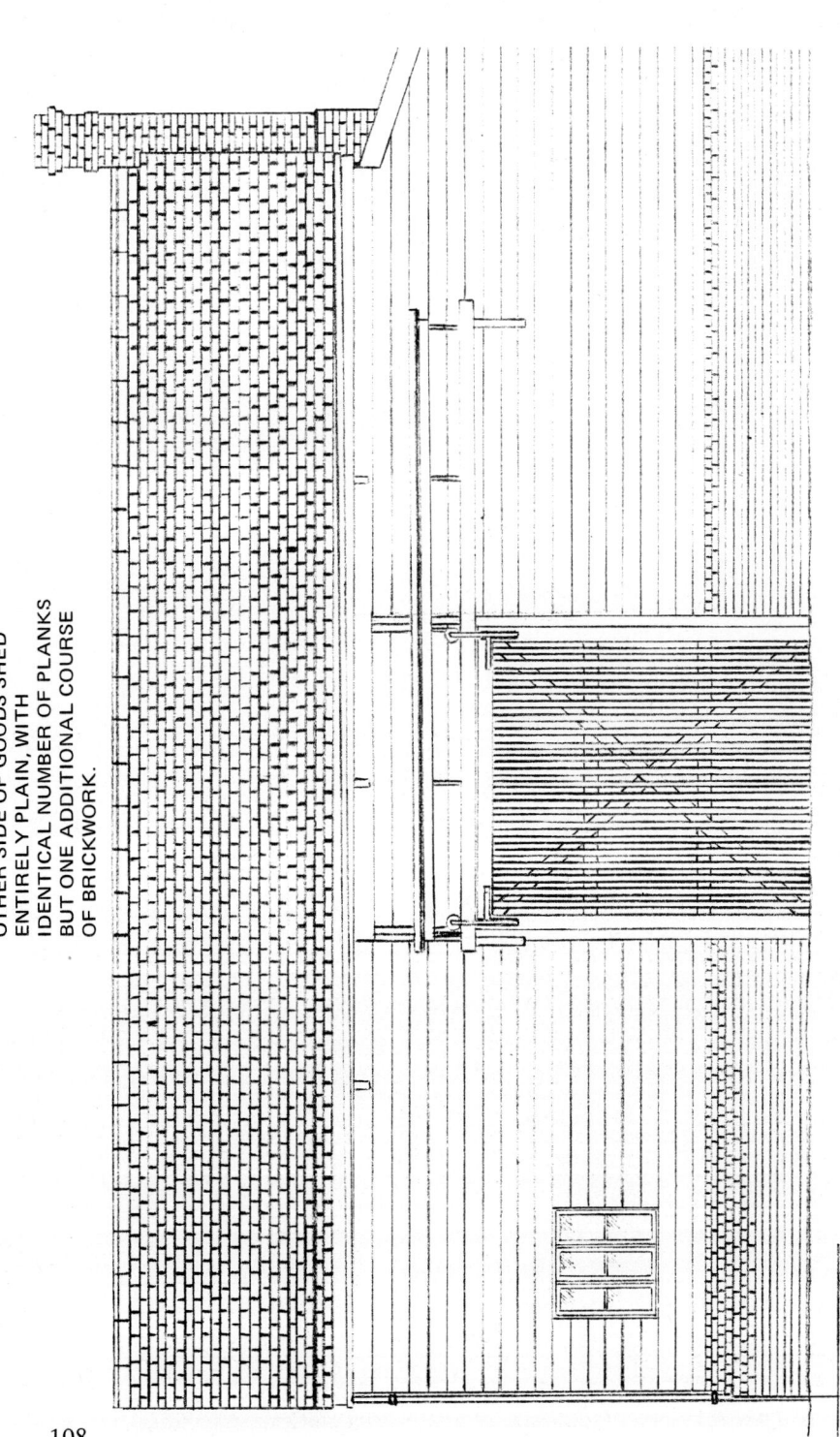

OTHER SIDE OF GOODS SHED
ENTIRELY PLAIN, WITH
IDENTICAL NUMBER OF PLANKS
BUT ONE ADDITIONAL COURSE
OF BRICKWORK.

108

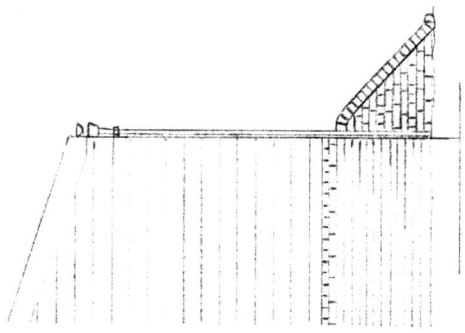

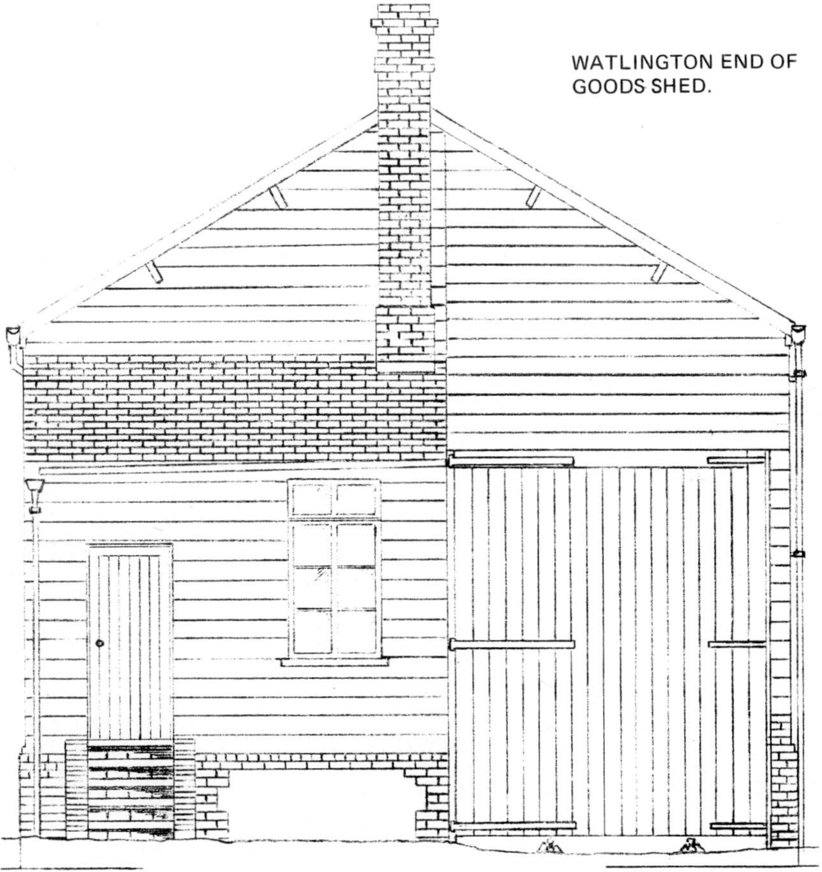

WATLINGTON END OF
GOODS SHED.

Watlington goods shed.   *(Courtesy P. Karau)*

Halt styles. Kingston Crossing (top) and Bledlow Bridge.

(Loco. & General Railway Photographs)

Princes Risborough from the North. Aylesbury bay, autotrailer alongside, on left. Watlington bay on right.

(British Railways)

VALUATION OF W. & P.R. RLY. STOCK
Agreed by Mr. J. Tomlinson & W. Dean, 2 August 1883, Paddington

1. Tank engine 2-2-2, Sharp Stewart	£220
2. Tank engine 2-4-0, Sharp Stewart	£850
1. Composite, Lancaster Wagon Co.	£185
1. Third, Lancaster Wagon Co.	£145
1. Passenger brake van, Lancaster Wagon Co.	£130
3 old carriages and 2 pairs of old wheels	£ 40
1. Open goods wagon	£ 24
2. Open goods wagon	£ 24
3. Open goods wagon	£ 24
4. Open goods wagon	£ 24
5. Open goods wagon	£ 24
6. Open goods wagon	£ 24
	£1,714

Timetable and Fares of the Watlington and Princes Risborough Railway, from "Bradshaw" for January - June 1873.

1st	2nd	3rd	Gov.		Gov.	Aft.	Aft.
—	—	—	—	Watlington	9.15	2.15	6.00
9d	6d	5d	3d	Aston Rowant	9.25	2.25	6.10
1s 3d	10d	8d	5d	Chinnor	9.35	2.35	6.20
2s 3d	1s 6d	1s 1d	9d	Princes Risborough	9.45	2.45	6.30
				Princes Risborough	10.05	3.35	6.43
				Chinnor	10.15	3.45	6.53
				Aston Rowant	10.25	3.55	7.03
				Watlington	10.35	4.05	7.13

"Metro" class 2-4-0T No. 615 worked on the Watlington branch in 1909.

"2021" class 0-6-0T No. 2026. By 1928 when it first appeared at Watlington, the inelegant combination of saddle tank and extended smokebox shown here had given way to pannier tanks of more conventional appearance.

No. 2159, penultimate engine in the class, was the first to be recorded from Watlington in pannier tank guise – as depicted here with open cab and backplate.

No. 2069 was allocated to the branch during 1929 and 1931, and exemplifies the "2021" series in final form, with closed cab and Swindon extended bunker.

(Loco. & General Railway Photographs)

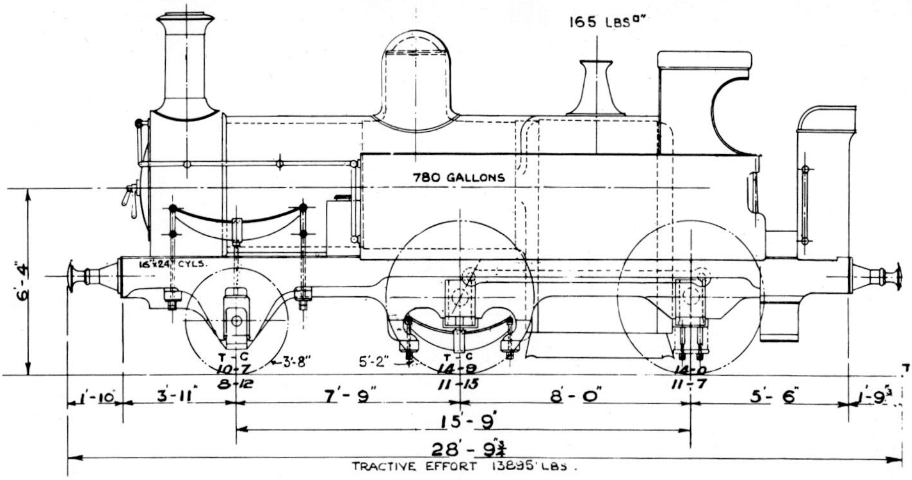

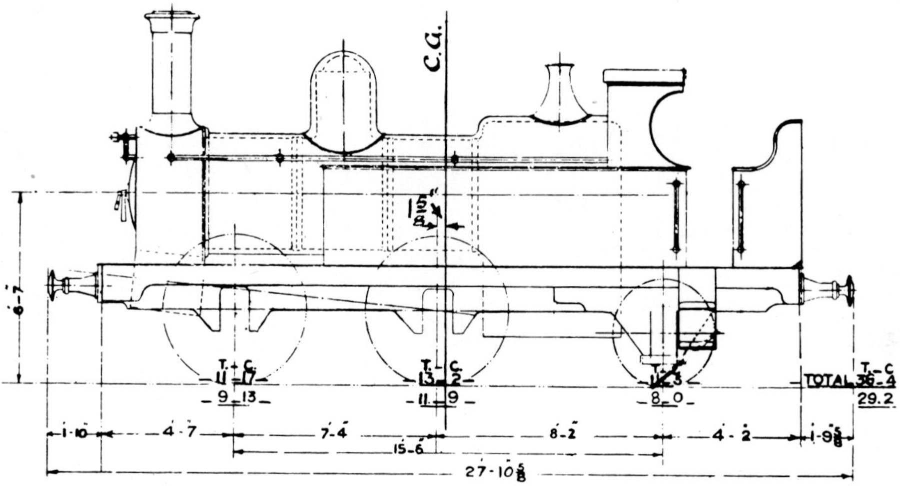

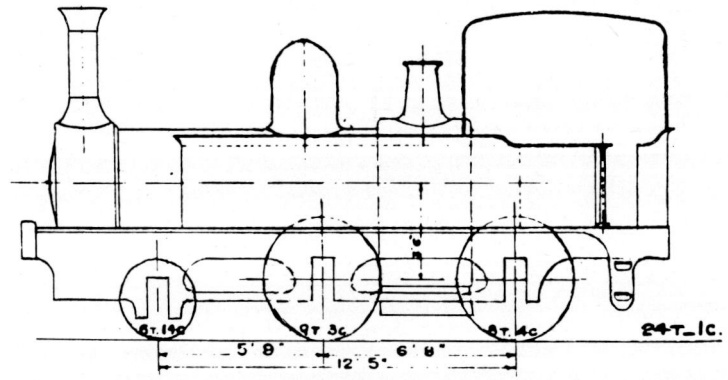

"Small Metro" class (top), "517" class (above), and GWR diagram for No. 1384.

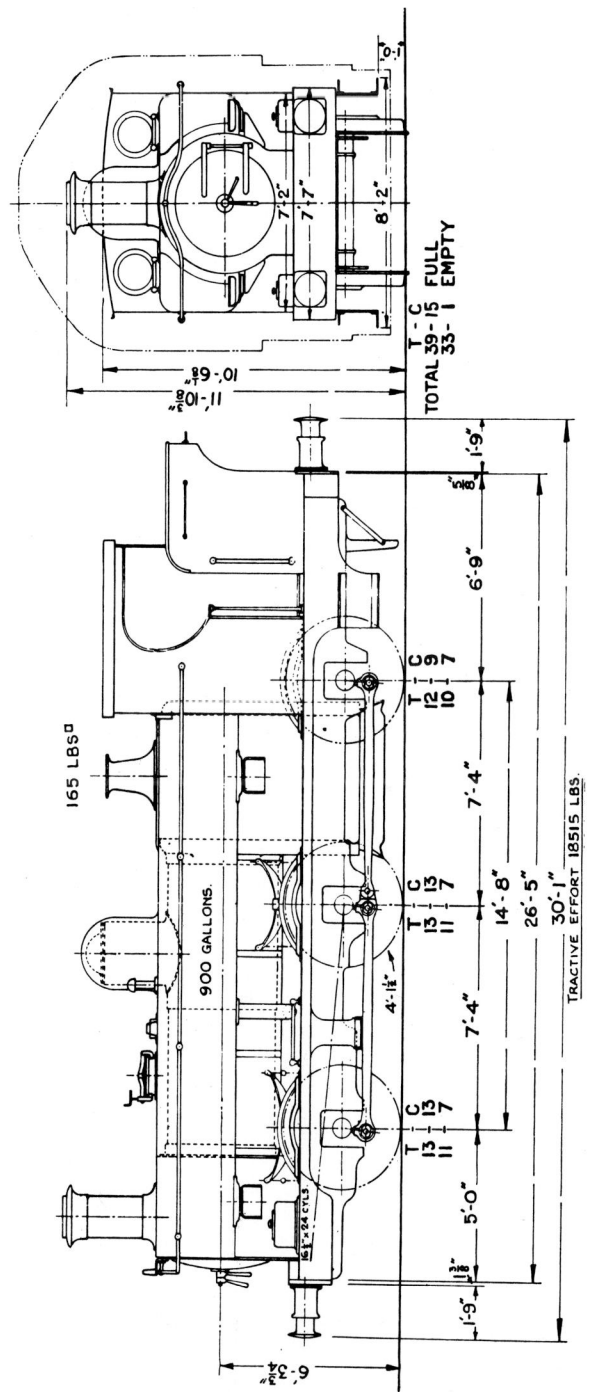

"2021" class 0-6-0T in later condition with pannier tanks, enclosed cab and extended bunker.

12' 1 1/16"
84·5
8' 4"
58·5
8' 2"
57
11' 3 13/16"
79
1'9"
12
6' 2 5/8"
43·5
5' 2"
36
8' 3"
58
5' 2"
36
7' 9"
54
3' 8"
26
4' 0"
28
1'9"
12
6' 4"
44·5

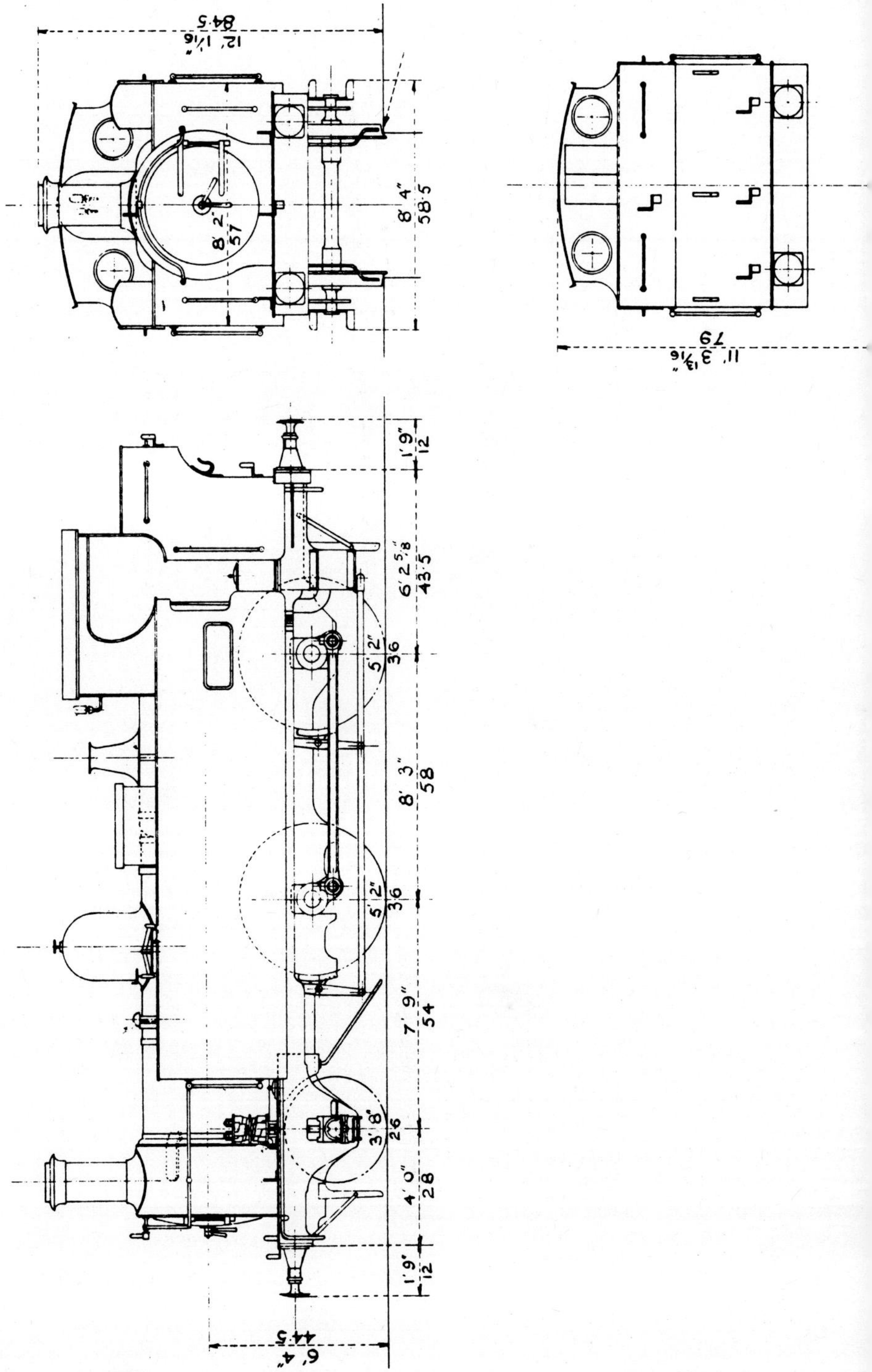

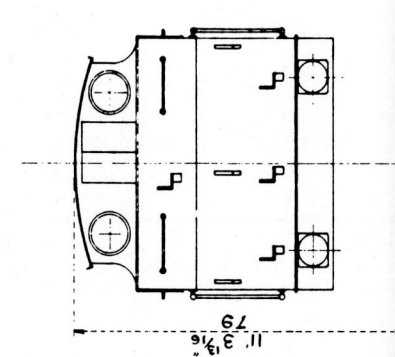

Tickets

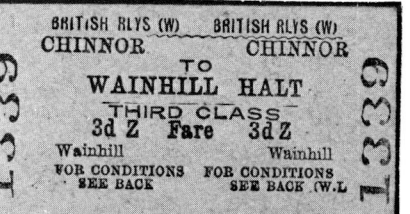

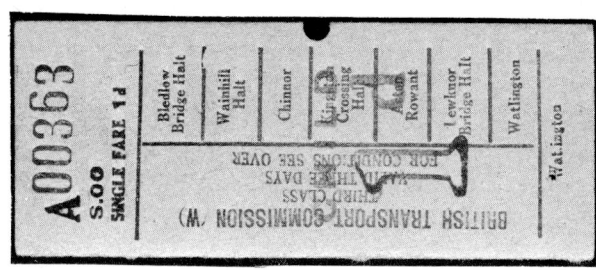

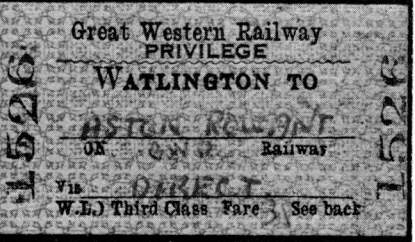

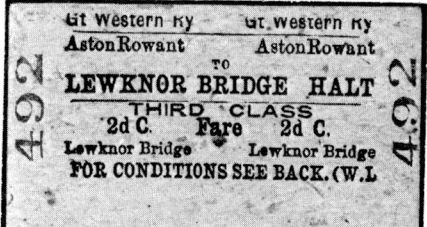

Notes